W9-AUB-795

The
Tiananmen
Square
Massacre

Other books in the At Issue in History series:

The
Tiananmen
Square
Massacre

Kelly Barth, *Book Editor*

Daniel Leone, *President*
Bonnie Szumski, *Publisher*
Scott Barbour, *Managing Editor*
James D. Torr, *Series Editor*

 AT ISSUE IN HISTORY

**GREENHAVEN
PRESS®**

San Diego • Detroit • New York • San Francisco • Cleveland
New Haven, Conn. • Waterville, Maine • London • Munich

© 2003 by Greenhaven Press. Greenhaven Press is an imprint of The Gale Group, Inc.,
a division of Thomson Learning, Inc.

Greenhaven® and Thomson Learning™ are trademarks used herein under license.

For more information, contact
Greenhaven Press
27500 Drake Rd.
Farmington Hills, MI 48331-3535
Or you can visit our Internet site at http://www.gale.com

LIBRARY OF CONGRESS CATALOGING-IN-PUBLICATION DATA

Tiananmen Square massacre / Kelly Barth, book editor.
    p. cm. — (At issue in history)
Includes bibliographical references and index.
ISBN 0-7377-1175-2 (pbk. : alk. paper) —
ISBN 0-7377-1176-0 (hardback : alk. paper)
    1. China—History—Tiananmen Square Incident, 1989. I. Barth, Kelly. II. Series.
DS779.32 .T556 2003
951.05'8—dc21
                                                                2001008517

Printed in the United States of America

Contents

mise even with liberal leaders, a move that probably would have prevented bloodshed.

Foreword

Historian Robert Weiss defines history simply as "a record and interpretation of past events." Both elements—record and interpretation—are necessary, Weiss argues.

> Names, dates, places, and events are the essence of history. But historical writing is not a compendium of facts. It consists of facts placed in a sequence to tell a connected story. A work of history is not merely a story, however. It also must analyze what happened and *why*—that is, it must interpret the past for the reader.

For example, the events of December 7, 1941, that led President Franklin D. Roosevelt to call it "a date which will live in infamy" are fairly well known and straightforward. A force of Japanese planes and submarines launched a torpedo and bombing attack on American military targets in Pearl Harbor, Hawaii. The surprise assault sank five battleships, disabled or sank fourteen additional ships, and left almost twenty-four hundred American soldiers and sailors dead. On the following day, the United States formally entered World War II when Congress declared war on Japan.

These facts and consequences were almost immediately communicated to the American people who heard reports about Pearl Harbor and President Roosevelt's response on the radio. All realized that this was an important and pivotal event in American and world history. Yet the news from Pearl Harbor raised many unanswered questions. Why did Japan decide to launch such an offensive? Why were the attackers so successful in catching America by surprise? What did the attack reveal about the two nations, their people, and their leadership? What were its causes, and what were its effects? Political leaders, academic historians, and students look to learn the basic facts of historical events and to read the intepretations of these events by many different sources, both primary and secondary, in order to develop a more complete picture of the event in a historical context.

In the case of Pearl Harbor, several important questions surrounding the event remain in dispute, most notably the role of President Roosevelt. Some historians have blamed his policies for deliberately provoking Japan to attack in order to propel America into World War II; a few have gone so far as to accuse him of knowing of the impending attack but not informing others. Other historians, examining the same event, have exonerated the president of such charges, arguing that the historical evidence does not support such a theory.

The Greenhaven At Issue in History series recognizes that many important historical events have been interpreted differently and in some cases remain shrouded in controversy. Each volume features a collection of articles that focus on a topic that has sparked controversy among eyewitnesses, contemporary observers, and historians. An introductory essay sets the stage for each topic by presenting background and context. Several chapters then examine different facets of the subject at hand with readings chosen for their diversity of opinion. Each selection is preceded by a summary of the author's main points and conclusions. A bibliography is included for those students interested in pursuing further research. An annotated table of contents and thorough index help readers to quickly locate material of interest. Taken together, the contents of each of the volumes in the Greenhaven At Issue in History series will help students become more discriminating and thoughtful readers of history.

Introduction

Beijing's Tiananmen Square is located directly south of the entrance to the Forbidden City—the home of the imperial palace of the old capital of China. *Tiananmen* translates as "Gate of Heavenly peace" in English. In China's long history Tiananmen Square has been the site of numerous significant political events. In June of 1989, it became the focal point of one of the bloodiest scenes of political strife China has ever witnessed.

Beginning in April, college students and eventually citizens from around the country occupied Tiananmen Square in protest of many of the Communist Party of China's (CPC) policies. The demonstrators called for several broad political reforms: freedom of the press and of speech, economic growth, an end to political corruption, increased funding of education, and a move toward democracy. Ultimately thousands were killed or injured after the government sent military troops into the area in an attempt to quell the antigovernment protests. The international community was shocked at the news images of prodemocracy protestors fleeing soldiers equipped with machine guns and tanks.

The Legacy of Communism

To understand the reason for the student protest, it is necessary to put it in historical perspective. By the late 1980s, CPC officials had realized that China needed major economic reforms in order to compete on the world market. In the late 1970s the government had already made a significant step toward reform by gradually dissolving China's agricultural communes (farms operated by Chinese citizens under compulsion by the government). These agricultural communes had been established during the Cultural Revolution—the period between 1969 and 1979 in which the government, under Communist leader Mao Zedong, tried to impress upon all citizens the importance of putting the needs of the Chinese people as a whole above their own individual welfare.

10

After the communes were abandoned at the end of the Cultural Revolution, the government encouraged the former farm workers to develop their own businesses in rural areas. In the 1980s, the CPC attempted to encourage similar entrepreneurship in urban areas, but with less success. It was difficult to discourage people's dependence on state-owned businesses. Furthermore, when the party stopped regulating the prices of goods and services and instead allowed businesses to set their own prices, prices soared and widespread inflation resulted. Political corruption increased as well, with politicians accepting political bribes and favors from people who wanted them to do things that would help them personally.

Divided Leadership

The Chinese leaders' disagreements over how to rule the country and manage its economic problems added fuel to the fire that would eventually burn in Tiananmen Square. The leaders were essentially divided over whether to maintain strict ideological and political control over the country and its citizens as the Communist Party had done in the past or make moves toward more liberal policies.

On one side of this divide were Hu Yaobang and Zhao Ziyang, two reformist-minded party members who called for loosening of government control over the economy. They were staunchly opposed by a group of political leaders known as the Eight Elders. The Eight Elders believed that if the government loosened its ideological control, Chinese society would begin to crumble. They clung to the four principles of maintaining a stable government that their leader, Deng Xiaoping, had established in a famous speech he made in 1979: 1) adherence to socialism, 2) the dictatorship of the proletariat, or working class, 3) the leadership of the CPC, and 4) faithfulness to the tenets of Marxism-Leninism and the teachings of Mao Zedong. The Elders feared Hu Yaobang's approach would lead to what they called "bourgeois liberalism," or what Americans would call capitalism or a free market economy.

Though officially a member of the Eight Elders, Deng Xiaoping tried to maintain an awkward middle-of-the-road position in the conflict over how to rule China. On the one hand, he supported Hu's economic reforms, but on the other, he strongly believed, with the Eight Elders, that the country must strictly adhere to the basic tenants of communism.

As a result of these internal differences within the party and the halting reforms they instituted, China's economic problems only worsened. Local political leaders became corrupt, using loopholes within the new economic system and accepting bribes in exchange for political favors. Average workers whose basic needs had been met under the stricter Communist system were now falling through the cracks as a result of the party's reforms.

The military, in particular, suffered from these mismanaged economic reforms. Because funding the military was no longer a government priority, weapons became outdated and deteriorated and military installations were robbed and vandalized. Also, the military was still indoctrinated with ideas that directly conflicted with the country's new emphasis on individualism and a free market economy. Soldiers were still taught to uphold the former style of government, which promised financial security for all who contributed to society. Historically underpaid, some members of the military had hoped to take advantage of the dissolution of state-run farms by developing their own livelihoods as farmers. However, they came into conflict with rural people who saw them as unnecessary competition. The government did little to assist soldiers in finding other jobs, and the country began to lose its once widespread respect for the military.

As time went on, Chinese citizens themselves began to force the party to address these problems. In 1986, students held antigovernment demonstrations in Beijing and other major cities. The Politburo, the party's main governing body, forced Hu Yaobang to resign from his position as party general secretary and assigned him the blame for what they considered the ideological weakening of the country. Deng Xiaoping also tightened regulations and promoted the distribution of increasingly rigid Communist ideological propaganda to shore up the party's ideological hold over China.

Ridding the party of Hu did not solve the party's disagreements. In Hu's place stepped Zhao Ziyang, another politically moderate party general secretary who maintained that Hu's ideas of reforming Communist ideology and continuing political liberalization would stimulate China's economy. Despite the anti-liberalization stance of the Eight

Elders, Deng wanted new party secretary Zhao to be able to continue economic reform.

To speed up economic reform, Zhao headed up a new Politburo committee called the Small Group to Research Reform of the Central Political System. Acting on the advice of economists, Zhao and his committee set about to dismantle the existing system of state-set prices for major products. This decision backfired. Fearing that prices would skyrocket once they were no longer regulated by the government, people panicked and bought up goods before the new policy went into effect. Disappointed with the results of Zhao's ideas, Deng curbed his economic reform plans and lost confidence in him.

Citizens Protest for Reform

Anxious about low wages and poor living conditions, many people began to believe that antigovernment protests were the way to shed light on bad governmental policies. Even though they made up only a small proportion of the young people in the country, college students took the lead in expressing this widespread loss of faith in communism that so alarmed party leaders. A survey was conducted at twenty-three Beijing colleges and universities by the State Education Commission and delivered in report form to the Central Committee of the Communist Youth League in March of 1989, just months before the Tiananmen Square protest began. The survey revealed a widespread belief that Marxist and Leninist thought could no longer be applied in a country moving toward reform. Instead, students wanted a combination of socialism—a system of government that still reflected concern for its citizens—and capitalism.

Any government attempt to control the rising tide of dissatisfaction fell by the wayside with the death of Hu Yaobang on April 15, 1989, which galvanized the burgeoning student movement for protest. Early on, students were careful only to mourn Hu Yaobang in their marches in the square, which the party said was a legal reason for assembling in public, but then a small number of students began to take Hu's funeral as an opportunity for an antigovernment protest. The students requested a meeting with party officials to express their concerns, and when party officials refused, protestors began a sit-in at the Great Hall of the People beginning April 18. In the CPC-controlled media, the students were depicted as dangerous. Premier Zhao Ziyang initially encouraged the party to maintain restraint when dealing with the students, maintaining that the students would soon return to classes. However, he also encouraged students to leave Tiananmen Square and warned that those who did not could be prosecuted.

Student protesters from fifteen universities formed an organization they called the Autonomous Federation of Students (AFS) and issued the following list of actions they insisted the party take before they would leave the square. Among the demands were that the party: 1) affirm Hu Yaobang's views on democracy, 2) admit that party campaigns against bourgeois liberalization had been wrong, 3) publish the incomes of state leaders, 4) end the ban on privately run newspapers and free speech, 5) increase education funding and teacher pay, 6) end restrictions on public demonstrating, and 7) hold elections for the positions held by existing party leaders.

The effects of the antigovernment protests were felt not just in Beijing but all across the country. Students from other large cities such as Shanghai, Nanjing, and Wuhan held their own protests. As the days wore on, the protests became increasingly embarrassing to party leaders, who had to find a way to contain the situation without making villains out of the students. Official reports blamed a few outside instigators for riling up the students with false information and encouraging them to protest. When the protesters read government reports saying that they were being manipulated by a few antigovernment individuals, students set out to prove them wrong. They moved from just mourning Hu to conducting unveiled protests critical of the government. On April 23, just one day after Hu's memorial service, students and faculty from universities across China boycotted classes. Student protesters in Beijing ousted the party-sanctioned student organization from their government offices and installed themselves there.

On April 26, Deng Xiaoping wrote an editorial for the *People's Daily*, the main party newspaper, condemning the protests in Tiananmen Square as unpatriotic. Both students and, increasingly, common citizens took offense at Deng's criticism of the protests, which they believed to be for the good of the country.

Chinese Leaders Debate How to Handle the Protests

The party leadership became increasingly divided over how to handle the protests. Consistent with his conciliatory tone throughout, Premier Zhao Ziyang called for Deng to retract his harsh editorial. Zhao tried to hold a middle ground between students and the government. Zhao believed that since the reforms the students were calling for were already being called for within the party as well, the protests were generally positive and could be resolved peacefully while keeping the Communist party intact. Deng sharply disagreed with Zhao's approach to the students and the rift between them grew.

Finally, on May 13, student protesters from Beijing University resorted to a hunger strike to try to force party leaders to have a dialogue with them. The protestors also demanded that this dialogue be broadcast on state television for the entire country to see. Though they softened toward a dialogue, CPC leaders said they would not allow it to be televised.

Nearly a month after it began, the protest began to draw the support of intellectuals and the country's working class as well. On May 15, a group of about 100,000 of these ordinary citizens took to the square in protest of party policies. The party was further embarrassed during Russian president Mikhail Gorbachev's visit on May 16, in which he met with Deng Xiaoping at the Great Hall of the People, a building in plain view of the square and the thousands of protesters.

Far from giving in to student demands, government leaders began talk of instituting martial law to bring the hunger strike and the protests to a close. When on May 18, the leaders of the Politburo Standing Committee met to discuss martial law, Zhao Ziyang submitted his resignation as premier. The students feared that if Zhao was no longer in power, they could be in real danger of the government taking military action against them.

Martial Law Is Declared

Because the Politburo Standing Committee members remained divided on martial law, the Eight Elders decided to take matters into their own hands, and alone they voted to institute martial law. Following the meeting, Li Peng and Zhao Ziyang finally met with students in the square. Zhao urged them to leave peacefully, assuring them that eventually their demands for political reform would be met. Fearing that violence could no longer be averted, he wept and said the government should have negotiated sooner.

On May 19, when martial law was declared in Beijing, soldiers faced fierce opposition from citizens, who blocked the streets to prevent them from entering the square. Justifiably concerned, AFS warned the 300,000 protesters in the square to prepare to disband should the People's Liberation Army (PLA) enter the square. Over the next several days, train stations all over the country were flooded with students trying to join the protests in Beijing.

Meanwhile, party leaders discussed how they would handle the protesters and resolve the situation. Most of all they wanted to maintain the fragile remains of the Chinese people's trust and loyalty, and their decisions reflected that. For example, they chose Jiang Zemin, the party leader in Shanghai, to replace Zhao Ziyang as premier, instead of Li Peng, who would have been next in line for the position but who was very unpopular with the public as a result of his harsh condemnation of the protests. Zhao and his close friend and secretary Bao Tong were put under house arrest for their failure to squelch the movement.

By the end of May, the situation had reached a boiling point. Party leaders felt they must plan military action not only to prevent violence against the troops in the square but also to remove the protesters from it. A small but tenacious group of about one-hundred student protesters remained in the square. On May 29, their spirits were bolstered when students from the Central Academy of Fine Arts in Beijing wheeled in a statue they called the Goddess of Democracy, which looked like the Statue of Liberty. Protesters wanted to hold out until the meeting of the National People's Congress on June 20, where they believed the government would be forced to address some of their demands.

They could not have known that the government and the PLA were already planning to move on the square. On June 1, Li Peng issued an emergency document, "On the True Nature of the Turmoil" aimed at establishing the legitimacy of clearing the square by force. On June 2, the Politburo Standing Committee decided to begin the military crackdown.

The Crackdown Begins

Neither the soldiers nor the government could have been prepared for the enormous resistance that ordinary citizens offered the troops headed for Tiananmen Square. Deng's instructions said that there was to be no bloodshed; that would not be the case. When soldiers entered the suburbs surrounding Beijing, they encountered roadblocks and angry citizens armed with sticks, bottles, rocks, and handmade weapons. People took over PLA buses and formed human walls to prevent them from moving toward the square. Frightened soldiers first fired rubber bullets into the crowds. When this had little or no effect, soldiers fired real bullets, killing many. Most of the deaths occurred on Fuxingmenwai Boulevard, a main road through the western suburbs of Beijing.

By the early hours of June 4, tanks filled with soldiers had finally made their way through the streets to the square. Though initial reports indicated that soldiers fired on student protesters, it was later learned that protesters had finally evacuated peacefully at 5:40 A.M. However, thousands of people lay dead or injured in the streets of Beijing. The PLA and the Chinese Communist Party quickly regained control over Beijing and the country at large, putting to rest any remaining fears that the existing government would be overthrown.

After the Crackdown

In the years since the uprising, China's economic system has expanded a great deal, but its political system has changed little. Many of the same rules and constraints in place at the time of the student uprising are still in force today. Though China's current leaders certainly do not want to repeat the events of June 1989, they still have not officially expressed regret for the former leaders' actions or made significant changes in their policies concerning freedom of speech and other human rights issues. Many of the protesters involved in the Tiananmen Square movement have either been extradited to other countries or are still being held in prison for their actions. The causes of the Tiananmen protests, the circumstances surrounding the Chinese government's crackdown, and the legacy of the Tiananmen Square Massacre are debated in the following volume.

Chapter 1

The Roots of
the Massacre

1

The Chinese Government's Opposition to Reform

Liu Binyan

In the following selection, Liu Binyan argues that the Tiananmen protests and subsequent crackdown resulted from the Chinese leadership's unwillingness to institute genuine social and political reforms. By April of 1989, he writes, the economic situation in China had reached a crisis point. The Communist Party leaders had instituted some liberal economic reforms, including relaxed control over the prices for goods and services and increased competition between businesses. However, these reforms lead to skyrocketing prices, increased corruption at all levels of government, and widespread fear and distrust of the Chinese Community Party. Public discontent was exacerbated by the fact that although the country's highest ranking elder Deng Xiaoping had initiated economic reforms, he refused to allow social and political reforms. When student protesters openly called for freedom of the press, civil liberties, and democratic elections, Deng called them anti-patriotic. In his mind, to question the Communist Party was to be disloyal to it, and disloyalty could not be tolerated.

Liu Binyan wrote this article just a few months after the Tiananmen Square Massacre. One of China's best-known journalists, Liu Binyan was in the United States on a Nieman fellowship at Harvard University when the Tiananmen Massacre occurred. Angered by his written critiques of the crackdown, the Chinese Community Party did not allow him to return to China. He still lives and works in the United States.

Excerpted from "Deng's Pyrrhic Victory: China After Tiananmen Square," by Liu Binyan, *New Republic*, October 2, 1989. Copyright © 1989 by The New Republic, Inc. Reprinted with permission.

D eng Xiaoping regards the massacre at Tiananmen
Square as a great victory. Hundreds of thousands of
dissident students and their supporters were brought under
control, and order was restored to the streets of Beijing.
The truth, of course, is that the uprising was the greatest
show of democratic force in over 40 years of Communist
rule in China. It gave the Chinese people confidence in
their strength and exposed the deep rifts within the Party
leadership. The movement ended with the old ruling clique
returning to the old political system but its grip on the
country is more feeble than ever. The extraordinary power
and potential of China's democracy movement is now clear.
When Hu Yaobang, the reformist-minded Party secretary,
was ousted from office in 1987, the student movement on
university campuses retreated. Many thought that the students, demoralized and temporarily defeated, had lost interest in politics, and that there would be no more large-scale
demonstrations. No one foresaw the events precipitated by
Hu's death this year [1989]. On April 16 a small number of
students gathered at Tiananmen Square to place wreaths in
his honor. By April 22, 200,000 students had defied a ban to
carry out a demonstration of mourning, with over 100,000
onlookers expressing sympathy. Afterward, over 300,000
students petitioned the government through hunger strikes
and peaceful demonstrations, winning the support of over a
million people, including intellectuals, workers, entrepreneurs, and ordinary citizens—an unprecedented event in
Communist China. The students' political maturity could
be seen in their organizational discipline and rationality.

In sharp contrast are the isolation, weakness, hypocrisy,
and brutality of the Communist rulers. Two general Party
secretaries have been dismissed within two and a half years.
And it was only by forcing every provincial Party committee to declare its support for the dismissal of Zhao Ziyang
and the appointment of Jiang Zemin that the top central
leaders were able to gain the formal majority necessary to
pass this measure. These leaders themselves are largely controlled by "eight senile retired emperors," all over 80 years
old, who do not hold formal office in the Party or government but who prop up their rule through brute force and
lies. Deng and his cohorts have lost the confidence of the
Chinese people and thus the legitimate right to rule. Americans often ask whether the Chinese people's demands for

democratic reform spring from the influence of Western culture. It is true that during the reform era many books were published that discuss Western society and political thought; that the return of foreign educated students has spread democratic thinking in society; and that the Chinese people have been exposed to Western culture through the mass media. But these influences alone never could have brought about such an enormous movement. Tiananmen Square was the inevitable result of a fundamental breakdown in China's internal political, economic, and social structure. Since the beginning of the reform and open-door policies in 1978 and 1979, the Chinese economy has grown rapidly. The new agricultural system gave the peasants (who constitute 80 percent of the population) incentives to increase production; and the growth of local enterprises and the influx of foreign capital and technology prompted rapid industrial expansion. The flourishing of free markets brought about a rise in people's standard of living.

Economic Reform Was Not Without Problems

But economic growth was accompanied by an explosion of social and political problems. Deng Xiaoping not only repeatedly refused to carry out political reform, he tried to whittle down the few freedoms people did enjoy. Economic reform ran into all kinds of bureaucratic obstacles, and the Party rectification campaign, aimed at stemming the tide of corruption and the degeneration of Party ethics, ended in failure. Graft and embezzlement and other uses of public office for private gain became rampant at all levels of government. Serious crimes increased rapidly, and official profiteering [went] wild. By 1983 the crisis was evident; by 1985 it had become pervasive.

The ouster of Hu Yaobang and the anti-bourgeois liberalization campaign in 1987 created more anger and despair, as did the soaring inflation. Chinese intellectuals, rooted in a tradition of serving the nation as a natural duty, adopted an attitude of silent protest against a series of Party-orchestrated political campaigns, including the anti-spiritual pollution [anti-religion] campaign and the anti-bourgeois liberalization [anti-democracy] campaign. Then last February [1988] three groups of intellectuals signed open letters addressed to the authorities demanding human rights. Two months later university students—who are least bound by traditional thinking, and haven't lost their vigor and their sense of Justice—resolutely marched from their campuses in mourning Hu's death.

One doesn't have to look far to discover how this crisis came about. Deng Xiaoping was attempting to promote economic reform while stubbornly insisting on upholding the "Four Principles" (the socialist path, the leadership of the Communist Party, the dictatorship of the proletariat, and Marxism-Leninism and Mao Zedong thought). His opposition to "bourgeois liberalization" and his desire to preserve Mao's overarching ideological and political framework were clearly at odds with his economic goals. It was inevitable that eventually either economic reform would break through the old political order, or the old political order would act as a brake on economic reform.

Deng Not a Reformer

Henry Kissinger, among others, likes to point out that it was Deng who initiated the idea of reform in the first place. *Time* magazine even selected him twice as Man of the Year. It's hard to reconcile the image of a leading advocate of reform with that of the executioner who crushed the democratic movement and then formed an alliance with those who had been the harshest critics of his policies. But Deng is a pragmatist, not a reformer. This is the man who in the 1960s noted that it doesn't matter whether the cat is white or black—if it catches mice, it is a good cat. After his return to power in 1978, faced with an economy devastated by the "Gang of Four," he resolved to dismantle the Maoist economic structure and introduce practical reforms that would arouse people's enthusiasm for production. This did require courage and spunk. At the time the conservatives were very influential. Some provincial Party committees simply refused to go along with the new policies; others adopted a wait-and-see attitude.

Deng Controls Those in Political Disagreement

In Deng's efforts to cross old ideological boundaries, he urged Hu (then chairman of the Organization Department of the Central Committee) to redress the cases of those falsely accused of political crimes during the Cultural Revolution, and to rehabilitate intellectuals who had been labeled as rightists during the anti-rightist campaign of 1957. These measures gained him widespread support. He subsequently encouraged Hu to initiate the debate over the slogan "Practice as the sole criterion of truth," which was a guiding principle of the reform ideology and established a more solid theoretical justification for modifying the orthodox Maoist economic system. The object of these actions was not to radically revamp the system, but simply to strengthen Chinese Communist Party rule, to prevent rebellion by those whose political consciousness had been raised during the Cultural Revolution [period during 1960–70s when intellectuals were sent to work on farms or as laborers], and to consolidate Deng's power within the Party. The real test of his zeal for reform came with the Democracy Wall movement. In the fall of 1978 political associations began to spring up spontaneously, and people from all over the country posted large posters on a wall near the Xidan intersection in Beijing. They discussed the lessons of the Cultural Revolution, criticized Mao's mistakes, and demanded democracy for China.

Leaders had the gall to say that . . ."we are dealing with the dregs of society and a gang of rebels who want to subvert our country and throw out our Party."

The next spring Deng cracked down on the movement (Wei Jingshen, one of its leaders, is still in jail). At about that time he issued the slogan "Uphold the four principles, and oppose bourgeois liberalization," an indication that he meant to preserve Maoist ideology. He could tolerate and even encourage attempts to correct the ideological mistakes in the Party only as long as his political power was not fully consolidated. As soon as his position was secure, and his economic reform policies under way, he reverted to a conservative ideology and politics.

To Deng, as to Mao, people are nothing more than instruments: in wartime they serve as soldiers; in peacetime they are hands for production. The common belief of both leaders is "If I conquer the mountain, then it is I who sits on the mountain." ("I" is the Party, which fought for power and thus has the legitimate right to it.) Only they can give orders, and the people must be docile and obedient.

People had gained a certain degree of economic freedom from the reform and open-door policies, but when they demanded democratic political rights, these were denied on the grounds that "the Four Little Asian Dragons [Hong Kong, South Korea, Singapore, and Taiwan] did not carry out democratic reform, yet they nevertheless made great economic progress." When people express dissatisfaction, the rulers accuse them of "picking up the bowl to eat meat, and putting it down to curse their Mother." When hundreds of thousands of people shouted, "Deng Xiaoping resign," at Tiananmen Square, the leaders had the gall to say that "it is not just the case of a few individuals who cannot distinguish right from wrong, but we are dealing with the dregs of society and a gang of rebels who want to subvert our country and throw out our Party."

Despite his supreme position, Deng of course did not act alone. Those who have significant influence over him include Party elders Chen Yun and Po Yipo, who have made every effort to derail economic reform; Hu Qioamu and Deng Liqun, who stubbornly uphold Maoist ideology; Peng Zhen and Li Xiannian, who favor "old people's politics" and refuse to retire; and Wang Zhen and Yang Shangkun, who cling to a superstitious belief in military force. It was inevitable that Deng would be influenced by this faction. Having spent much of his life in the military, he too has an almost mystical confidence in the power of the military. With the help of these ossified ideologues, he destroyed the reform project that he created. They all refuse to see that the political system is destroying itself from within.

Causes of Inflation

The Tiananmen conflagration could not have been started without the sparks of inflation and government corruption. There were three factors that led to China's crippling rate of inflation. The first is the so-called "buying power of social groups." This peculiarly Chinese phenomenon refers to the fact that the spending not only of government departments and all state enterprises, but of companies, Party organs, and certain social groups supported by the state, are paid for with public funds. Since the Maoist era, there have been repeated injunctions to restrict the spending power of these groups. But not only was the government unable to bring the spending under control; the spending has increased every year.

According to figures published by the State Statistical Bureau, in 1977 social groups spent a total of 13.4 billion Chinese yuan; by 1988 spending had reached 66.5 billion yuan, and the national budget deficit had reached massive proportions. And as a reporter for the Xin Hua News Agency pointed out, these figures take into account only spending that is officially recorded; if "black market" spending was included, the figure would be up to about 100 billion yuan. With a GNP of around 200 billion yuan, the tremendous impact of this type of spending on inflation is self-evident.

Most journalists and employees in the judicial system and financial departments have long known about the illegal behavior and many have struggled to expose it.

The second factor is the scope of capital investment. Mao called for a development strategy based on reduced capital investment, but he never pulled it off. The reason is that the leaders of each province, city, and local government, as well as the heads of departments under the Party's Central Committee, all want their region to be the most developed. The scale and quality of an official's development projects serve as a record of his achievements, and the greater his "family property"—i.e., the size and scope of production in his home district—the greater his own power. In 1987 there was a campaign to cut this kind of wasteful investment, but it still ended up 30 percent higher than in 1986. Forty percent of this went to paying employee salaries and benefits, thus directly stimulating consumption, thus raising prices.

The third factor is China's bloated bureaucracy. For 40 years it has expanded, becoming an increasingly parasitic entity. Under Mao numerous campaigns were launched for "better staff and streamlined administration," but the bureaucracy only got bigger. In 1983–84 Deng made his own attempt, but he too failed. The number of public officials in

Party and government organizations has increased from 1.8 million in 1957 to 27 million [in 1989]. In the last several years, lower level government departments were given greater autonomy. Though intended to decrease the number of personnel, this had the opposite effect, and it raised the costs of production. State enterprises and the rapidly growing number of administrative "companies" have derived the greatest benefits from the relative freedoms of economic reform, and they have become those most actively engaged in speculation and profiteering. The resulting inflation has directly undercut the achievements of reform.

Corruption Flourishes

All three of these elements are tied to the existence of an elite bureaucratic class. Chinese bureaucrats are neither supervised nor subject to legal constraints. This class emerged during Mao's era but was limited in scale, and with the government's frequent political campaigns and tight economic control, its members were afraid to be too unscrupulous. After 1977, with the gradual loosening of Party control, corruption flourished along with the new economic freedoms.

The Chinese economy, which is 90 percent "publicly" owned (the so-called ownership by the whole people), is in fact controlled by this privileged bureaucratic class. It holds a virtual monopoly over raw materials, energy supplies, transportation, communication facilities, and financial resources. These bureaucrats wield tremendous authority, but because they are not held personally responsible for production levels, the abuse of public office is rampant. Those in newly emerging enterprises have to proffer gifts, banquet invitations, and bribes to obtain capital and resources. The stealing and selling of economic information for personal gain is common and even the children of officials engage in malfeasance.

Many officials have worked in the same location since land reform in the 1950s. They have long-standing relations with their superiors and former colleagues and war companions, and a vast network of friends and family. In one county in Hebei province, a county magistrate embezzled 2,000 yuan. He was not of very high rank, and the sum was not significant, but when the central government sent a team to investigate, 800 people came to testify in his behalf.

Judicial System Is Corrupt

The independent judicial process has totally broken down: those who pervert Justice for a bribe are not punished by law, and those who shirk their duties are not apprehended. The higher an official's rank, the safer he is from punishment. As long as he has a "behind-the-scenes supporter," he is guaranteed not to be reprimanded for illegal behavior. In legal cases involving officials or their relatives, the real criminals are protected, and the innocent are punished.

In 1983 the Central Committee initiated Party rectification. But after two years the campaign ended in failure. According to the *People's Daily*, 100,000 Party members of all ranks were kicked out for infractions of discipline and illegal activities. Yet only about 30 officials, of relatively low rank, were among them. No higher-ranking officials were included, let alone at the Central level.

In early 1986 Hu Yaobang convened an enlarged Party conference of 8,000 cadres calling for a continuation of the campaign and a determination to deal with "critical" cases, i.e., high-level officials. But not only were these cases not dealt with; Hu himself was forced to resign a year later. Since then a trend of "reversing verdicts" has set in, with those accused of illegal activities making a big fuss about having been the victims of the "bourgeois liberalization," and being absolved of all wrongdoing. Most journalists and employees in the judicial system and financial departments have long known about the illegal behavior and many have struggled to expose it. But the offenders are protected under the banner of "safeguarding stability and unity" and "opposing bourgeois liberalization," promoted by Party committees at all levels. Still, the witnesses to corruption, though powerless to stop it, remember it. They have shifted over the years from disappointment to despair, from dissatisfaction to fury. Most have settled for passive resistance: some are indifferent; others are cynical, engaged only in pleasure-seeking; some engage in work slowdowns, or are merely perfunctory in their work. Throughout the population, however, there are those who have found their own means to redress their grievances. In 1985 and 1986 students launched their series of protests. At the same time disruptive social behavior was on the rise, and criminal cases were increasing at a rate of 30 percent to 40 percent a year. Meanwhile, the bureaucratic monopoly over the supply of fertilizer and diesel oil, which allowed officials to sell through the black market at high prices, created fury among the peasantry. In February 1987 a researcher in charge of agricultural policy revealed that the scale of peasant demonstrations had far surpassed that of the student demonstrations in 1986. But because of the vast country side, the isolation and dispersion of the peasants, and the restraints on the flow of information, the society remains largely ignorant of these events. Recently in Hu Lan County in Manchuria, the "Hu Lan Robin Hood" appeared—a person who specializes in killing policemen known to be brutal and corrupt. The inhabitants of a nearby county posted a large sign saying, "We welcome the Hu Lan Robin Hood to carry out an investigation in our County." Organizations have sprung up whose goals are to "bring peace out of chaos" and to kill the rich and distribute the wealth.

What will be the Party's next step? Deng recently called for the continuation of reform and open-door policies, and for a new leadership, which is supposed to make people believe that "the situation is hopeful, that reform is still being pursued." He has also called for those guilty of corruption to be punished, for "ten to 20 serious cases of corruption to be tried as showcases," as proof of the government's determination to deal seriously with the problem. But he has also been saying that "the four principles are fundamentally sound," that if any problem exists, it is because they "have not been upheld thoroughly enough," and that the suppression of bourgeois liberalism and spiritual pollution should be more actively undertaken."

The People Lose Confidence in Government

After the massacre of Tiananmen Square, the Deng-Li-Yang clique (Deng Xiaoping, Li Peng, and Yang Shangkun) lost the last shred of the people's confidence. The nationwide wave of arrests has thrown the country into a white terror even more frenzied than during the Cultural Revolution. Even as Deng professes to want to continue reform policies and crack down on corrupt officials, he labels scholars and students "counter revolutionary elements."

Since the Communist Party came to power, its authority has been absolute, encompassing every aspect of people's private lives. The rulers have refused to countenance any constitutionally guaranteed rights: freedom of the press,

elections for people's representatives, an independent judicial process. They demand that people obey orders and
maintain "unity with the Party." They have refused all demands for people's supervision over the Party, claiming that
the Party can correct its own mistakes. People may have believed such lies in the 1950s and 1960s, but ten years of the
Cultural Revolution and ten years of reform have height-
ened their political consciousness, as the angry shouts of the
thousands on the Square testified.

---

*After the massacre of Tiananmen Square, the
Den-Li-Yang clique (Deng Xiaoping, Li Peng,
and Yang Shangkun) lost the last shred of the
people's confidence.*

Since then, the schisms within the Party organization
from the highest level down to the grass roots have become
even more apparent. Many Party members have publicly resigned, among them influential intellectual elites. Disillu-
sionment within the Chinese diplomatic community abroad
has been steadily increasing. Fewer and fewer young people
are looking to join the Party. The control of the central
leadership over the local and grass-roots Party organizations, and the control of the Party organization over Party
members, is steadily weakening. As the leaders' impotence
has become manifest, they have resorted to increasingly fascist methods. They now must coerce Party organizations at
every level into demonstrating their support and loyalty,
compelling cadres and intellectuals to make declarations of
unity with the Party.

Meanwhile, productivity has fallen drastically, and government departments are in a state of semiparalysis. Peasants have been refusing to sell their products because the
state purchasing price is so low and the government often
does not even have the cash to buy them. The Li Peng government has discovered that guns can temporarily suppress
a democratic movement but cannot solve pervasive economic and social problems.

The life expectancy of this government cannot be long.
No one expects its successor to be a truly democratic one.
Nor is it certain that it will abandon the self-destructive

ways of the old men [the Eight Elders] now ruling the country. But it is clear that the Chinese people are no longer lulled by disingenuous promises of reform. For three or four days after the Tiananmen Square massacre university students in cities all over the country continued to demonstrate. The government crackdown gave birth to an underground resistance movement. In greater numbers and with renewed determination, people will continue to organize, and to pursue their struggle through both legal and non-legal means.

2

Reforms Were Impossible Under Communism

George Jochnowitz

George Jochnowitz is an American who was teaching English in China at the time of the Tiananmen massacre. In the following selection, he contends that by 1989, many Chinese people had begun using bribes and graft to get the goods, services, and opportunities that they wanted. They felt guilty for doing so: They believed they had succumbed to the capitalist mentality of acquiring possessions at all costs, an ideology that communism had warned them to avoid. Jochnowitz, however, argues that it was not the lure of capitalism, but rather the fundamental flaws of communism that led to such widespread corruption. The kinds of changes the protesters were calling for in Tiananmen Square—including economic reform and a reduction of corruption in government—were not possible within a Communist system. Though students would never have said they wanted to overthrow the Communist government during the protests, that, in essence, is exactly what they were calling for.

My family and I first taught at Hebei University in Baoding, China during the spring semester of 1984. My younger daughter and I returned five years later, in February of 1989. We wanted to return for a number of reasons: to see old friends again, to improve our Chinese, to see whether China was changing as much as people said it was.

Excerpted from "The Words of Marx, the Methods of Lenin," by George Jochnowitz, *National Review*, August 4, 1989. Copyright © 1989 by National Review Inc. Reprinted with permission.

Between 1984 and 1989, our whole family had pursued our interest in China. We all read lots of books about China and talked to the Chinese students we knew from Baoding and elsewhere who were studying here. It seemed clear: something big was happening in China, and I wanted to see it for myself. Had I known just how big, I wouldn't have gone.

Shanghai and Peking looked brighter and richer than I remembered them, but Baoding was to be the real test. I love Baoding, but I have to admit it is ugly and very dull. Yet there was no question: even in drab old Baoding things were different. To begin with, there were doorbells. When we visited an old friend and rang her bell, it played the first eight bars of Beethoven's "Fur Elise." Apartment interiors used to look like service stations, unpainted concrete with minimal furnishings. Now there were bright colors, carpets, decorative objects, and occasionally musical instruments. Clothing was bright too, and Mao jackets were no longer common. A boy and a girl might walk together; they might even hold hands! Best of all, people were willing and sometimes even eager to talk about politics.

Mixed Feelings Among the Chinese

Our own living standards had gone up. We had a television, a refrigerator, rugs, and hot water in the morning as well as in the evening. There was no running water at night and no electricity on Sundays, but we were used to that. We remarked to everyone how much better things were than in 1984. Few people agreed. The "back door" had become the major topic of conversation. It is common wisdom that jobs, college admissions, medical care—just about everything of importance—depends on connections, supplemented by gifts and occasionally outright bribery. "We are very evil people," everyone says. "We love nothing but money. We cultivate friendships so we can get in through the back door. We used to be good, but now we are selfish, just like you." Some people say this in deep shame, others with open delight and pride, most with a mixture of the two sentiments.

"Were you better people when you turned your mothers in to the police for counterrevolutionary thoughts?" I asked maliciously. Everybody loved me for it. They enjoyed hearing me say bad things about their system, though their complaints were not the same as mine. They were tired of being poor, but they felt China was becoming capitalist and therefore selfish and immoral.

Many Chinese believe capitalism is the source of the wealth and power of the West and the secret to achieving a society as rich as America's. But believing capitalism will make everybody rich and happy is not the same as thinking capitalism is good. Goodness under Mao was equated with sacrifice and suffering; therefore, the wish to make China prosperous is selfish and immoral.

The problem with Mao Zedong was not that he misunderstood Marxism but that he understood it very well.

One of the new words that had come into use in China since my last stay was *guandao*, meaning "corrupt officials." Corruption, alas, is found in all sorts of societies. It is especially prevalent, however, in one-party states, where it is sheltered by the lack of political opposition. It is also likely to flourish where there is no independent press to hunt it down. It is easy for us Americans to grow annoyed with partisanship and scandal-hunting, but in China, where the Party and the press are the same as the government, guandao are built into the system.

The government, to be sure, complains about guandao, asks citizens to report them, and punishes them with great severity. Indeed it is in the interests of the government for the people to believe that all their problems come from corrupt individuals rather than from a system that by its nature leads to corruption and protects it.

College in China, as in America, lasts for four years, generally from the ages of 18 to 22. There were about forty English majors at Hebei University every year. In addition to teaching linguistics courses, I taught conversation to the freshman and composition to the seniors. It was hard to mark forty papers a week, but it gave me a chance to learn what my students were thinking. The first theme I asked them to write was on the topic "My Dream." About half the seniors dreamed of being assigned the job of their choice. In China, graduates are assigned jobs by their university, a practice I consider not only inhumane but counterproductive, since people stuck for the rest of their lives in positions they hate are not likely to be efficient workers. That suggested the topic for the second composition: "The Policy of Job Assignment." Some students argued that job assignment was a major source of corruption; others maintained the policy was necessary because if students looked for their own jobs, back-door practices would get even worse.

The third essay I asked for, needless to say, was "The Back Door." The compositions tended to be quite pessimistic, with some students saying that the problem reflected a flaw in the Chinese character. I would rather think it is a reflection of flaws in the Chinese Communist system, where there is no front door since there are no rights.

Baoding was richer, more cheerful, and freer than before, but it disapproved of itself. This in itself was evidence of improvement. Disapproval and doubt can frequently be constructive forces, leading to a search for solutions and consequently to new analyses.

Change Not Possible Under Marxism

When people start to think, they disagree. Everyone may have considered corruption China's greatest problem, but some felt the answer was a return to Maoist purity and others began to talk of legal systems. It was exciting and even intoxicating to be in a country where so many people thought so much and so seriously about their society. But there was one idea very few were ready to entertain—the thought that the evils of a Marxist society could possibly come from the writings of [Karl] Marx himself.

Liu Binyan, a daring reporter expelled from the Party for his attacks on guandao, is a typical example of the bold thinker who is not bold enough. Writing in the January 18, 1989, issue of the *New York Review of Books*, he said, "The socialism imported from the Soviet Union and implemented in China was not true socialism. From [Joseph] Stalin [Soviet Communist leader] to [Communist leader of China from 1949–1976] Mao Zedong, we have had false Marxism."

The problem with Mao Zedong was not that he misunderstood Marxism but that he understood it very well. Marx looked forward to an era without merchants and therefore without specialization, when one would "rear cattle in the evening [and] criticize after dinner." This is entirely consistent with closing the schools and exiling professionals to the countryside; Mao was not misinterpreting Marx.

When Hu Yaobang [former leader deposed for his "liberal" ideas] died, somehow everyone knew there would be an embarrassingly large outpouring of mourners at his memorial service on April 22. It was the occasion everyone had been waiting for.

Big-character posters appeared on campus shortly after April 22, not only to provide first-hand reports of the activities at Tiananmen Square, but to stimulate discussion. Poems and essays were written and posted, and copied down by other students in their notebooks. The tiny minority of those who were willing to question Marx ceased to be tiny, although it remained a minority. The atmosphere grew ever more intoxicating.

On May 13 [1989] the hunger strike began in Tiananmen Square. Somehow that was a catalyst: more and more thoughts began to cross the line; Marx was replaced by Patrick Henry, Thomas Jefferson, and Martin Luther King. Never had I expected to see a Chinese student in Tiananmen Square with a headband bearing the English words, "I have a dream." Others crossed different lines, breaking different taboos. Mao buttons suddenly appeared out of nowhere, both in Baoding and in Peking.

When workers joined the demonstrations, a success few had dared to hope for, the students lost their ideological nerve. No one wanted to shatter the unity that had suddenly appeared. Those demonstrating for due process and separation of powers stood side by side with those who admired Mao; together they faced down the army in the wee hours of May 21 and held control of Peking.

"You have won," I told my Chinese friends. "The army has disobeyed."

"The army will never disobey," they replied. "This is China."

"But it already has." I countered. "And there are demonstrators not only in Tiananmen but in Baoding. It's not the same China it used to be."

Totalitarian Societies Inhibit Change

My Chinese friends were right. The Chinese government is not designed to respond to public opinion. There is no way orderly change can occur in a totalitarian society. There can be nothing but power struggles and coups. The students were not ready to break down the walls of the Zhongnanhai compound, where China's rulers live, and kill or arrest its residents. Deng Xiaoping, on the other hand, was ready to kill or arrest the students, and he did.

Deng, for ten years, had worked to make China prosperous. At the same time, he had put down the Democracy Wall movement, imprisoned dissidents, and suppressed free thought. As a Chinese, he wanted his country to be rich; as a Communist, he insisted that it remain true to its Marxist ideology. When he had to choose between China and the Party, he chose the Party.

What can the pro-Mao members of the democracy movement be thinking now? Maoism is back with a vengeance. Deng's speeches are being read and studied, the country is being saturated with lies, and citizens are being called upon to report their loved ones to the police. Deng is above all a Communist. He once said, "It doesn't matter what color the cat is, as long as it catches mice," but he was lying. He once said, "Seek truth from facts," but he was lying. For Deng, truth means the words of Marx and the methods of Lenin.

On the afternoon of June 4, a few hours after the Tiananmen massacre, a group of students left the campus of Hebei University to hold a march through Baoding. They had done so many many times since the funeral of Hu Yaobang. But this time there was a new slogan, one that would have been impossible a mere 12 hours earlier: Da dao Gongchan Dang (Down with the Communist Party). . . .

Deng Xiaoping, Li Peng, and their colleagues are cornered rats. They must kill and lie merely to stay alive. They cannot simply retire; they are too hated for that. On June 4 and 5 (the day my daughter and I left Baoding) people were saying, "Kill them. Hang them." In his June 9 [1989] speech, Deng said the demonstrators' "real aim was to overthrow the Communist Party and topple the socialist system." That aim was implicit in their quest for honesty, order, and kindness, but nobody said so before the massacre and perhaps only a minority of the students thought so. It was Deng himself who made them say so. Da dao Gongchan Dang!

3

Deng Xiaoping Condemns the Tiananmen Protesters

Deng Xiaoping

One of the Eight Elders and China's most respected leader, Deng Xiaoping strongly believed that the Tiananmen Square protests threatened to throw China into political turmoil. In the following editorial, published several weeks prior to the government's crackdown on the protesters, Deng states his belief that the students are not the masterminds behind the protest movement. Instead, he believes that a small number of people seeking to overthrow the Communist Party and its leaders have manipulated the students into protesting during their legitimate mourning of the death of the popular liberal leader Hu Yaobang. He emphasizes that the primary reform the students are calling for—a democratic government free of corruption—is the goal of the Chinese Communist Party as well. If the protests continue, he warns, the government's pursuit of reform will be jeopardized. Deng condemns the student movement as a threat not only to the survival of the Communist Party, but to all of China as well.

In their activities to mourn the death of Comrade Hu Yaobang, communists, workers, peasants, intellectuals, cadres, members of the People's Liberation Army and young students have expressed their grief in various ways. They have also expressed their determination to turn grief into strength to make contributions in realizing the four

From "It Is Necessary to Take a Clear-Cut Stand Against Disturbances," by Deng Xiaoping, *Renmin Riboa*, April 26, 1989. Translation copyright © 1990 by M.E. Sharpe, Inc. Reprinted with permission.

modernizations and invigorating the Chinese nation.

Some abnormal phenomena have also occurred during the mourning activities. Taking advantage of the situation, an extremely small number of people spread rumors, attacked party and state leaders by name, and instigated the masses to break into the Xinhua Gate at Zhongnanhai, where the party Central Committee and the State Council are located. Some people even shouted such reactionary slogans as, Down with the Communist Party. In Xi'an and Changsha, there have been serious incidents in which some lawbreakers carried out beating, smashing, looting, and burning.

Taking into consideration the feelings of grief suffered by the masses, the party and government have adopted an attitude of tolerance and restraint toward some improper words uttered and actions carried out by the young students when they were emotionally agitated. On April 22, before the memorial meeting was held, some students had already showed up at Tiananmen Square, but they were not asked to leave, as they normally would have been. Instead, they were asked to observe discipline and join in the mourning for Comrade Hu Yaobang. The students on the square were themselves able to consciously maintain order. Owing to the joint efforts by all concerned, it was possible for the memorial meeting to proceed in a solemn and respectful manner.

Small Number Take
Advantage of Students' Grief

However, after the memorial meeting, an extremely small number of people with ulterior purposes continued to take advantage of the young students' feelings of grief for Comrade Hu Yaobang to spread all kinds of rumors to poison and confuse people's minds. Using both big- and small-character posters, they vilified, hurled invectives at, and attacked party and state leaders. Blatantly violating the Constitution, they called for opposition to the leadership by the Communist Party and the socialist system. In some of the institutions of higher learning, illegal organizations were formed to seize power from the student unions. In some cases, they even forcibly took over the broadcasting systems on the campuses. In some institutions of higher learning, they instigated the students and teachers to go on strike and even went to the extent of forcibly preventing students from going to classes, usurped the name of the workers' organizations to distribute reactionary handbills, and established ties everywhere in an attempt to create even more serious incidents.

An extremely small number of people with ulterior purposes continued to take advantage of the young students' feelings of grief for Comrade Hu Yaobang.

These facts prove that what this extremely small number of people did was not to join in the activities to mourn Comrade Hu Yaobang or to advance the course of socialist democracy in China. Neither were they out to give vent to their grievances. Flaunting the banner of democracy, they undermined democracy and the legal system. Their purpose was to sow dissension among the people, plunge the whole country into chaos and sabotage the political situation of stability and unity. This is a planned conspiracy and a disturbance. Its essence is to, once and for all, negate the leadership of the CPC [Communist Party of China] and the socialist system. This is a serious political struggle confronting the whole party and the people of all nationalities throughout the country.

Disturbance Must Be Stopped

If we are tolerant of or conniving with this disturbance and let it go unchecked, a seriously chaotic state will appear. Then, the reform and opening up; the improvement of the economic environment and the rectification of the economic order, construction, and development; the control over prices; the improvement of our living standards; the drive to oppose corruption; and the development of democracy and the legal system expected by the people throughout the country, including the young students, will all become empty hopes. Even the tremendous achievements scored in the reform during the past decade may be completely lost, and the great aspiration of the revitalization of China cherished by the whole nation will be hard to realize. A China with very good prospects and a very bright future will become a chaotic and unstable China without any future.

The whole party and the people nationwide should fully understand the seriousness of this struggle, unite to take a clear-cut stand to oppose the disturbance, and firmly preserve the hard-earned situation of political stability and unity, the Constitution, socialist democracy, and the legal system. Under no circumstances should the establishment of any illegal organizations be allowed. It is imperative to firmly stop any acts that use any excuse to infringe upon the rights and interests of legitimate organizations of students. Those who have deliberately fabricated rumors and framed others should be investigated to determine their criminal liabilities according to law. Bans should be placed on unlawful parades and demonstrations and on such acts as going to factories, rural areas, and schools to establish ties. Beating, smashing, looting, and burning should be punished according to law. It is necessary to protect the just rights of students to study in class. The broad masses of students sincerely hope that corruption will be eliminated and democracy will be promoted. These, too, are the demands of the party and the government. These demands can only be realized by strengthening the efforts for improvement and rectification, vigorously pushing forward the reform, and making perfect our socialist democracy and our legal system under the party leadership.

The Future of China Is at Stake

All comrades in the party and the people throughout the country must soberly recognize the fact that our country will have no peaceful days if this disturbance is not checked resolutely. This struggle concerns the success or failure of the reform and opening up, the program of the four modernizations, and the future of our state and nation. Party organizations of the CPC at all levels, the broad masses of members of the Communist Party and the Communist Youth League, all democratic parties and patriotic democratic personages, and the people around the country should make a clear distinction between right and wrong, take positive action, and struggle to firmly and quickly stop the disturbance.

4

The Tiananmen Protesters' Declaration of a Hunger Strike

Autonomous Federation of Students

After repeatedly requesting a meeting with top Chinese Communist Party officials in May 1989, the student protesters were becoming exasperated by the government's refusal to agree to a serious dialogue. Though lower-ranking government officials had talked with them, the students felt their demands and concerns were not being taken seriously by those actually able to effect the changes they were calling for. The demonstrators were also angered by Deng Xiaoping's editorial in the *People's Daily* newspaper, which dismissed the protests as a "chaotic disturbance." They also disagreed with Deng's insistence that the movement had been instigated by a small number of political rabblerousers who incited the students to protest, rather than by the students themselves. The students called for Deng to take back what he had said about them in the editorial, asking him to admit that the movement was both "patriotic and democratic" in nature and had the good of the country at heart. The following announcement of a hunger strike, prepared by the Autonomous Federation of Students (AFS)—the umbrella group governing student activities in Tiananmen Square—demonstrates just how serious the movement had become. The announcement caused great concern among Communist Party leaders, who saw it as a sign that they were losing political control over the situation.

Excerpted from "Declaration of a Hunger Strike," by the Autonomous Federation of Students, *The Tiananmen Papers*, compiled by Zhang Liang, edited by Andrew J. Nathan and Perry Link (New York: Public Affairs, 2001). Translation copyright © 1990 by M.E. Sharpe, Inc. Reprinted with permission.

In this bright, sunny month of [May 1989] we have begun a hunger strike. During the glorious days of our youth, we have no choice but to abandon the beauty of life. Yet how reluctant, how unwilling we are!

The nation is in crisis—beset by rampant inflation, illegal dealings by profiteering officials, abuses of power, corrupt bureaucrats, the flight of good people to other countries, and deterioration of law and order. Compatriots, fellow countrymen who cherish morality, please hear our voices!

The country is our country.

The people are our people.

The government is our government.

Who will shout if not us?

Who will act if not us?

Though our shoulders may be frail, though we are too young to die, we must leave, we have no choice. History demands this of us.

Our genuine patriotic fervor and peerless loyalty are dismissed as "turmoil." We have been accused of harboring "ulterior motives," and of "being exploited by a small handful of people."

Appeal to the People

We ask all honorable Chinese—workers, farmers, soldiers, ordinary citizens, intellectuals, celebrities, government officials, police, and the people who have fabricated the charges against us—to put your hands over your hearts and examine your consciences. Of what crime are we guilty? Are we really causing turmoil? We leave our classrooms, we march, we go on a hunger strike, we sacrifice our very lives. Yet our feelings are trifled with time after time. We endure hunger in our pursuit of the truth—for which we are beaten by the police. When our representatives kneel down to plead for democracy, they are ignored. Our demands for dialogue on equal terms are met with interminable delays. The safety of our student leaders is at risk.

What are we to do?

Democracy is the noblest human aspiration; freedom is a sacred human right, granted at birth. Today both must be bought with our lives. Is this fact something the Chinese people can be proud of?

This hunger strike has been forced upon us. We have no choice.

It is by a readiness to die that we struggle for life.

But we are children, still children! Mother China, look at your children. Hunger is destroying our youth. Can you not be moved when you see death approach us?

We do not want to die. We want to live, and live fully, because we are in the prime of our lives. We do not want to die; we want to learn all we can. Our nation is wretchedly poor. We don't have the heart to abandon our homeland through death. That is not what we seek. But if the death of a single person or of several people will enable a greater number of people to live better, or if these deaths can make our homeland stronger and more prosperous, then we have no right to live on in ignominy.

Dying for Democracy

Do not feel sorry for us, mothers and fathers, as we suffer from hunger. Do not feel sad, uncles and aunts, when we bid farewell to life. Our only desire is that the Chinese people enjoy better lives. We have but one request: Please do not forget that we did not seek death. Democracy is not the concern of only a few, and the building of democracy cannot be accomplished in a single generation.

It is through death that we await a sweeping and eternal echo.

Democracy is the noblest human aspiration; freedom is a sacred human right, granted at birth. Today both must be bought with our lives.

When a person is about to die, he speaks from his heart. When a bird is about to die, its cry is most plaintive.

Farewell, friends, take care. Loyalty binds the living to the dead.

Farewell, loved ones, take care. We don't want to leave you, but we must.

Farewell, mothers and fathers, please forgive us. Your children cannot be loyal citizens and worthy children at the same time.

Farewell, countrymen, let us repay our country in the only way left to us.

May the pledge that we write with our lives clear the skies in our republic.

Manifesto for a Hunger Strike

Dear countrymen, following up on our momentous demon-strations, today [May 13, 1989] we resolve to begin a hunger strike in Tiananmen Square.

Our reasons are:
1. To protest the government's indifference toward our boycott of classes;
2. To protest the government's labeling our patriotic, democratic student movement as "turmoil," and many distorted press reports.

We demand of the government:
1. Immediate dialogue—concrete, substantive, and on equal terms—with the Dialogue Delegation of Bei-jing College Students.
2. A fair and unbiased acknowledgment of the legiti-macy of the student movement, labeling it "patriotic" and "democratic."

Time for commencement of the hunger strike: 2 P.M., May 13 [1989].

Location: Tiananmen Square.

Battle cries:

"This is not turmoil. We demand redress!"

"Immediate dialogue! No more delays!"

"Fasting for the people—we have no choice!"

"International public opinion, please come to our aid!"

"World press, please support us."

"Democratic forces, please stand by us!"

5

Older Chinese Leaders Favored Martial Law

Deng Xiaoping et al.

As the student protests lingered well into the month of May, members of China's leadership still differed sharply as to how to handle the unrest. In marked disagreement were Deng Xiaoping, the elder whom younger leaders still looked to for guidance, and Party Secretary General Zhao Ziyang. While Zhao Ziyang believed peaceful negotiations with students would resolve the conflict in Tiananmen Square, Deng Xiaoping wanted to resort to martial law. Deng and his supporters accused Zhao of continuing to fuel the protests by giving the students hope for compromise on behalf of the Party. On May 17, when the Chinese Communist Party's ruling body, the Politburo Standing Committee, voted on whether or not to implement martial law as Deng suggested, Zhao resigned his post, but not before he and fellow Standing Committee member Hu Qili voted against martial law. Among the other Politburo Standing Committee members, Li Peng and Yao Yilin voted for martial law and Qiao Shi abstained. Angry with the Standing Committee's indecisiveness, the Eight Elders, a group of men who had formerly held offices in the Chinese Communist Party, declared an unprecedented meeting at Deng's home to press for consensus on the issue. Following are excerpts of the meeting minutes.

Deng Xiaoping [most influential of the Eight Elders]: "We old comrades are meeting with you today because we feel we have no choice. The Standing Committee should

Excerpted from "Elders Decide on Martial Law," by The Eight Elders and Members of the Politburo Standing Committee, *The Tiananmen Papers*, compiled by Zhang Liang, edited by Andrew J. Nathan and Perry Link (New York: Public Affairs, 2001). Translation copyright © 1990 by M.E. Sharpe, Inc. Reprinted with permission.

have come up with a plan long ago, but things kept dragging on, and even today there's no decision. Beijing has been chaotic for more than a month now, and we've been extremely restrained through the whole thing, and extremely tolerant. What other country in the world would watch more than a month of marches and demonstrations in its capital and do nothing about it? Comrades Chen Yun and Xiannian [two of the Eight Elders] came rushing back to the capital because of this, and all of us have been worried sick. I've discussed it with comrades Chen Yun, Xiannian, Peng Zhen [one of the Eight Elders], and others, and we all feel Beijing just can't go on like this; we have to have martial law. What's tricky is that we've never faced this kind of thing before: a small handful infiltrating into such a huge number of students and masses. It's hard to draw the lines between the camps, which has made it hard to do what we should have done long ago. Some comrades [namely, Zhao Ziyang and Bao Tong] in the Party think this is a simple question of handling students and masses. But in fact our opponents are exploiting this very perception in order to drag things out and try to wear us down. At bottom they want to overthrow our state and overthrow our Party—that's what's really going on here. If you don't see this point, you can't be clear about what's going on. If you do see it, then you'll know why we need martial law in Beijing.". . .

Zhao Ziyang Has Sharp Political Differences

Li Peng [Premier of the CCP]: "I resolutely support the wise plan for the implementation of martial law in the Municipality of Beijing proposed by Comrade Xiaoping and other Elders. I also want to say something about Comrade Zhao Ziyang. The reason Comrade Zhao Ziyang has not come today is that he opposes martial law. He encouraged the students right from the beginning. When he got back from North Korea, he came out with his May Fourth speech at the Asian Development Bank without clearing it with anyone else on the Standing Committee. The speech was drafted by Bao Tong, and its tone was completely different from the April 26 editorial's [Deng wrote to quell protest movement], but it got wide distribution and had a big propaganda impact. From then on we felt it was obvious that Comrade Zhao Ziyang's opinions were different from Comrade Xiaoping's and those of the majority of comrades on the Standing Committee. Anyone with political experience could see this, and certainly the ones causing the turmoil could also see it. Comrade Zhao Ziyang did show us in advance his remarks at the meeting on the seventieth anniversary of May Fourth, but he ignored the suggestion a few of us made that he must add 'oppose bourgeois liberalization' to that speech. The student movement escalated . . . and now we have a million people in the streets every day, and more coming in from outside Beijing. . . . Police have been on duty continuously for more than a month and are exhausted. So we completely support the implementation of martial law in Beijing.". . .

At bottom they want to overthrow our state and overthrow our Party—that's what's really going on here. If you don't see this point, you can't be clear about what's going on. If you do see it, then you'll know why we need martial law in Beijing.

Yang Shangkun [President of China]: "Comrade Zhao Ziyang asked me to request that his absence be excused today; he is suffering dizzy spells and has an irregular heartbeat and has gone to see a doctor. I have exchanged opinions with Comrade Zhao Ziyang many times. He has never been able to agree with the judgments of Comrade Xiaoping and members of the Standing Committee on the nature of the student movement and has wanted several times to change the judgment of the April 26 editorial. I have tried to advise him differently and have also criticized him. I have said that this is a huge problem and that to change the judgment would bring us all crashing down. The problem we now face is that the two different voices within the Party have been completely exposed; the students feel that someone at the Center supports them, so they've gotten more and more extreme. Their goals are to get the April 26 editorial repudiated and get official recognition for their autonomous federations. The situation in Beijing and the rest of the country keeps getting grimmer. So we have to guarantee the stability of the whole country, and that means starting with Beijing. I resolutely support declaration of martial law in Beijing and resolutely support its implementation.". . .

Wang Zhen [Vice President of China]: "These people are really asking for it! They should be nabbed as soon as they pop out again. Give 'em no mercy! The students are nuts if they think this handful of people can overthrow our Party and our government! These kids don't know how good they've got it! When we were their age we lived in a forest of rifles and a rain of bullets; we didn't know what a peaceful day was! So aren't they dandy, now? Give them peace and they don't want it; they want to go starve themselves instead. No appreciation! What do the Party and the government owe them? Our Party is the people's Party; our government is the people's government. Out of responsibility to our sacred motherland, and out of responsibility to the whole people, I resolutely support Comrade Xiaoping's wise decision on martial law. If the students don't leave Tiananmen on their own, the PLA should go in and carry them out. This is ridiculous!". . .

Students Suffer from Ideological Confusion

Hu Qili [Politburo Member]: "There are some things I need to think through here, and I want to consider carefully. But I'll follow Party discipline."

Qiao Shi [Politburo Member]: "For a long time now we haven't done a good job of implementing Comrade Xiaoping's Four Basic Principles and opposition to bourgeois liberalization, and the result has been a certain amount of ideological confusion. In recent weeks a tiny minority has taken advantage of ideological confusion, of the good intentions of many young students, of some mistakes of the Party and government, and of some corruption in our ranks to start plotting behind the scenes, creating turmoil, and scheming to use turmoil to reach its goal of denying Party leadership and the socialist system. I believe the time is now right for Party Central to declare martial law in some districts of Beijing. Once martial law is declared, the important thing is the threat that the army will represent. To take advantage of this threat, we must find the right moment to get the schools' Party and administrative leaders and faculty and some parents to remove the students from the Square. If we can do it this way, this would be the best way to solve the problem. We want to resolve the problem, not shed blood."

Chapter 2

The Crackdown

1

Bloodbath Reported in the Square

Louise Doder

Like many Western reporters, Louise Doder, a writer for *Maclean's* magazine, struggled to piece together what happened in Tiananmen Square on June 4, 1989. She, as well as the rest of the world, fully expected and assumed that the bulk of the killing took place right in the square, the site of the long antigovernment protest. Accordingly, the following report, written just days after the massacre, indicates that soldiers in China's People's Liberation Army fired into the crowds in the square, killing many student demonstrators in the process. Subsequent accounts would contradict this and many similar reports about massive student deaths in the square and redirect attention to the significant number of nonstudent protesters killed in the suburbs surrounding Beijing.

In the middle of one night last week, a group of students transported three huge pieces of plaster and wood—loaded on bicycles—into Beijing's Tiananmen Square. Forming a cordon against the secret police who tried to intervene, the rebellious students painstakingly put the sections together and erected an instant icon: a home-made, 35-foot-high replica of the Statue of Liberty. The students christened it the "Goddess of Democracy." But early on Sunday, what had been largely a peaceful mass occupation for four weeks changed dramatically when thousands of armed troops marched on the square, crushing the rebellion in a deadly showdown with the defiant demonstrators, and left a bloodbath in their wake. Said a crying worker, huddled in the square: "I have just had my last cigarette. We are going to die."

The troops forced their way into Tiananmen behind armored personnel carriers and tanks. They first fired off tracer bullets and tear gas, while loudspeaker messages warned the tens of thousands of students to leave. Then, they opened fire directly on the crowds and charged them with bayonets, killing—according to initial reports—hundreds of demonstrators, leaving hundreds of others wounded and causing mass panic. Some students responded by hurling ignited bottles of gasoline at the troops. Meanwhile, ambulances, their sirens wailing, carried most of the injured to nearby hospitals. Bicycles, pedicabs and city buses were also pressed into service to move the dead and wounded.

> *Then, they opened fire directly on the crowds and charged them with bayonets, killing— according to initial reports—hundreds of demonstrators.*

In the early stages of the showdown, the students had remained orderly and they swiftly threw up barricades, which the armored vehicles systematically smashed. They even managed to surround and burn two of the vehicles. But when the soldiers began firing randomly from all sides and from the roof of the Great Hall of the People on the western side of the square, fear and confusion spread. The huge crowds desperately sought safety in the side streets leading from Tiananmen, shouting "Bandits, bandits!" Even there, the troops continued to fire on them, as screams of terror filled the area. One man, who had been wounded and treated in a casualty ward—where he said the floor was inches deep in blood—added, "They were simply raking the crowd with bullets."

Army Hesitant to Control Protests

The massive military intervention clearly surprised the students and their supporters and suggested a long period of future instability. In the early stages of the intervention, the students showed remarkable courage in the face of the armed troops, and the army's ability to exert control without the use of extreme force seemed to be virtually nonexistent. When they first tried to invade the square on Saturday morning, the students scored a dramatic victory by forming a human barricade and turning the soldiers back with chants of "Are you human?" and "Do you have a conscience?"

The government was very definitely in control—and a massacre was the result.

But when the army started to return the next time, about 12 hours later, there was no turning back. And the line had been clearly drawn between the students and their supporters demonstrating for more democracy, and the forces of the conservative government of Premier Li Peng and the senior leader Deng Xiaoping. Said one woman protester, who claimed to be married to a soldier in the square: "The People's Army has become a fascist army, pointing guns at their own people." Added a hysterical man in Beijing's Shuili Hospital: "We can never forgive the Communist party for this."

The students' protest began with prodemocracy demonstrations following the death on April 15 of former Communist party chairman Hu Yaobang, whom they regarded as a reformer. It gained momentum in May when Soviet leader Mikhail Gorbachev arrived in Beijing—the first such visit in 30 years—and the students hailed him as a political revolutionary. On May 13, just two days before Gorbachev's visit, 1,000 students—the number later grew to 3,000—began a hunger strike on the square. By May 17, a million people had packed Tiananmen and the demonstrations spread throughout the country. But by the middle of last week, following the declaration of martial law on May 20, the number of students in the square had dropped to 2,000 tired and hungry protesters. Then the demonstrators hauled in the "Goddess of Democracy," and, later, the troops invaded.

The World Was in Shock

The terror in Tiananmen created sharp reactions in world capitals. President George Bush [Senior] said, "I deeply deplore the decision to use force against peaceful demonstrators and the consequent loss of life." In Ottawa, External

Affairs Minister Joe Clark called on the Chinese government to "cease its military action and to return to peaceful methods to resolve the current crisis." He added, "We greatly regret that, following a period of evident restraint, the Chinese authorities initiated the use of force."

The army's stunning and ultimately successful intervention was unexpected partly because earlier in the week there had been continuing signs of the government's reluctance to follow through on its earlier declaration of martial law and other stringent measures. The foreign media had widely ignored a government imposition of nearly a total news blackout. Authorities arrested and then released three union leaders after 2,000 people protested their detention. And when the government sponsored rallies against the uprising—at which marchers were reportedly paid to chant "Smash the traitorous bandits into little pieces"—the participants were decidedly unenthusiastic. But on Sunday morning in Tiananmen Square, it was the demonstrators and their statue that had been crushed. The government was very definitely in control—and a massacre was the result.

2

Soldiers, Not Protesters, Were Victims of Violence

Yuan Mu et al.

Just two days after the crackdown, Chinese Communist Party officials held a press conference for Chinese journalists to correct what the government viewed as rumors, errors, and misinformation put forth by protesters and foreign journalists. It was crucial for the party to regain the trust, respect, and obedience of the Chinese people if they were to maintain their tenuous hold on power. The following statements differ from other reports not primarily in terms of facts but in the interpretation of those facts. For example, party officials maintained that they squelched a rebellion instigated by a few "counterrevolutionary thugs" rather than widely supported antigovernment protests. Yuan Mu and his fellow officials do not deny that blood was shed, but they emphasize the deaths and injuries of soldiers over those of students and citizens. They admit responsibility for these civilian casualties, but they do not apologize for them. Instead they place the blame entirely on the people themselves for choosing to follow a few criminal instigators rather than the government.

Yuan Mu: Today we are holding a news conference for domestic journalists, not for [overseas] Chinese foreign journalists. The main reason for doing this is that since the early hours of the morning of June 3, a shocking counterrevolutionary rebellion, unprecedented in the history of the

Republic, has occurred in the capital. It has caused great concern to the media at home and abroad. Everybody is concerned about the event. Thus, the State Council asked Comrade Zhang Gong, political commissar and director of the Political Department of a certain martial law unit [video cuts to Zhang Gong in uniform]; Comrade Yuan Liben, secretary general of the Beijing Municipal Party Committee; Comrade Ding Wenjun, deputy secretary general of the Beijing municipal government [video cuts to Ding Wenjun], and myself to give to you information about this matter. [Video shows people seated at long tables in rows, cuts to show Yuan Liben seated on Yuan Mu's right. Camera moves to close-up of Yuan Mu.] After this, you may ask questions if you have any, and we will answer them as completely as possible according to what we know about the situation. To begin with, I would like to say a few things:

First, the current situation is that a very few thugs engineered a counterrevolutionary rebellion in the early hours of the morning of June 3, but because of the valiant struggle of the People's Liberation Army [PLA], they were not entirely successful—their plot for rebellion was not entirely successful. We have achieved the initial—or shall we say first-step—victory in crushing the rebellion. The rebellion has not been completely quelled, however. The situation in the capital remains very grim. This is a general description of the current situation after our study. . . .

Officials Estimate the Number of Casualties

Over 5,000 officers and men of the PLA have been wounded. Over 2,000 civilians, including the handful of lawless ruffians and the onlooking masses who do not understand the situation, have been wounded. As for the number of people who have died, our preliminary statistics, which are incomplete as I just said, show that nearly 300 people have died. This includes soldiers, bad elements who deserve this because of their crimes, and people who were killed by mistake.

Moreover, over 400 PLA officers and men are still missing. These figures are acquired from various martial law units. Their whereabouts are still unknown. We do not know whether they are dead or alive. As time goes on, or when the situation stabilizes, we may, through further investigation, establish that some are still alive and that some may have sacrificed themselves.

This is the general situation. I have repeatedly stated that these figures may not be very accurate. However, one figure is relatively accurate because it has been obtained from various colleges—we checked all colleges, one by one: As of now, twenty-three college students have been reported dead. This figure is more specific. All other figures are not very specific. They are just rough figures. They are not very accurate. I expect possible changes to these figures when things become clearer as the situation further develops or stabilizes. Since it is a question in everyone's mind, I therefore have opted to inform you comrades first

[Video cuts back to a medium close-up of Yuan Mu.] Another issue is the clean-up in Tiananmen for which I will give the floor to Comrade Zhang Gong in a short while as he was there when the troops cleaned up Tiananmen Square. There is also a tape recording which you can also view. The basic situation of the students' withdrawal from Tiananmen Square was peaceful [pauses, smiles, and chuckles]. Yes, a peaceful withdrawal.

[Interrupted by voice from off camera.] Voluntary withdrawal? [Yuan Mu half-turns to his left, smiles.]

Yuan: Yes, voluntary withdrawal. Peaceful withdrawal. But the students maintained that their withdrawal was peaceful. It was possible that both sides [words indistinct]. As for the specific conditions, Comrade Zhang Gong will brief you later on.

Beijing Is Still in Unrest

Another point is that the State Council maintains that the situation facing the capital is still very grim. Stabilizing the overall situation and the further restoration of public order are primary concerns regarding the capital's overall situation. The capital has a population of over ten million. If the situation further worsens and public order cannot be restored, it would give the extremely few rebels, the thugs, the extremely few thugs or bad people an opportunity which they can exploit to their advantage. [Attendant leans in front of camera, apparently placing microphone before Zhang Gong.]

According to the information gathered so far, they are still carrying on with various kinds of sabotage activities including beating, smashing, looting, and burning. [Video cuts to wide shot of hall, showing attendant moving microphones around Yuan Mu's table.] Buses are continuously being burned; roadblocks are being set up constantly. What is particularly serious is that we have been informed that they are planning to cut off the water and electric supply and further paralyze transportation. [Video cuts back to same medium close-up view of Yuan Mu.] . . .

The Media Must Unite the People

Therefore, we hope that all residents of the capital will join comrades of the PLA, armed police, public security cadres, and policemen in quickly restoring normal order to the capital. Some comrades have suggested that we may now raise a slogan saying that we should safeguard our life and safety. If our daily activities cannot be carried out as usual, the people's interests would be more difficult to protect. If the situation gets worse, if the conspiracies of those scoundrels who have harbored all kinds of hatreds against socialism and our country should succeed, and if these scoundrels do overturn the People's Republic of China by taking advantage of the current chaotic situation, then the problem would be more grave. I feel that there should not be any basic conflict of interest between our comrades of the PLA, armed police personnel, public security cadres and policemen, and the vast number of the masses. Their interests should be in line with each other's. Therefore, we hope our public media units, considering the overall situation, will do their best to prevent our internal problems from getting worse.

Let us join our efforts in maintaining order. By so doing, those illegal and riotous acts may be more clearly exposed and better handled, and social order may be restored more quickly. I wish to make it clear that we should not have mercy for those who planned the riots and those behind-the-scenes organizers of the riots, because the contradictions between them and us are of an antagonistic nature. If this is not clearly understood, and if this problem is not resolved, the interests of the great majority of the people cannot be safeguarded. I think the vast numbers of the masses, including the vast numbers of students, have expressed their support for communism and socialism since the beginning of the student strike. I think our country would not have a future if it does not have the leadership of the communists and if it does not take the socialist path. I think the great majority of the people of Beijing and the whole country have a common understanding of this.

Therefore, I hereby urge the public media to do their best to convey this signal in order to defuse all kinds of misunderstandings and to ease as many contradictions as they can. Let us join forces to achieve these goals. As I have said, the precondition for this is that the people, the military, the armed police, and public security personnel must unite. The most urgent thing, as mentioned in the Beijing municipal government's emergency notice, is that, in order to improve the current situation, the vast numbers of Beijing residents should not go out to the streets as onlookers in the current chaotic situation. They should just go to work and go home as usual, stick to their own posts, and should not stay too long in the streets. This is not a restriction of the people's freedom. The purpose of enforcing martial law is to restore normal order. Under the current conditions, the situation could be stabilized sooner if this advice is followed. If the situation is not stabilized, many things will be very difficult to carry out. Our reforms, construction, efforts to improve the economic environment and rectify the economic order, and our efforts to deepen reforms would become empty talk. So, we must first stabilize the situation. It is very, very important that everyone stay at his or her post, and do his or her share. . . .

The basic situation of the students' withdrawal from Tiananmen Square was peaceful.

Will Comrade Zhang Gong give a brief account on what has happened at Tiananmen, the work done to clean up Tiananmen Square, the enforcement of martial law by PLA units, and other things related to the martial law troops?

Zhang Gong: I am Zhang Gong.

Unidentified voice: How do you write your name?

Rumors Must Be Quelled

Zhang Gong: Zhang is the character composed of *gong* [bow] and *chang* [long], and Gong is the same character as used in the term *gongren* [workers]. First, I wish to explain a question to our comrades in the journalistic circles in a responsible manner. Through you, I also wish to see to it that the people in the capital and all other parts of the country can clearly understand the question I am going to explain. Between 4:30 A.M. and 8:30 P.M. on June 3, that is, at the time when our martial law unit was carrying out the task of cleaning up Tiananmen Square, the unit absolutely did not kill one single student or individual. No one was killed at that time. Nor was there a single person killed or injured because he was run over by our vehicle.

[Yuan Mu interposes as video shows him:] That is to say, no tank or military vehicle was used to run over people.

Zhang: No, not a single person was killed or injured because he was run over by our vehicle. At present, an allegation is being circulated in society; that is there was a so-called bloodbath at Tiananmen Square when the liberation army was cleaning up the square. Also, there is another allegation that many people were shot to death, and the corpses were burned in Tiananmen Square. This is a sheer rumor. Nothing like that has ever happened. I think this perhaps was fabricated by a very few people with ulterior motives. I hope that you will not believe this rumor.

[Zhang smiles, picks up a folded page from table, and unfolds it, and refers to the page.] Now there are many rumors. Incidentally, when I entered this hall a while ago, I was told that there is now a rumor which claims that our 38th Army Group and the 27th Army Group have been engaged in a vigorous fight for the Nanyuan Airport, that the fight has been continuing since last night, and that even artillery has been employed. [Turns to look behind, over his left shoulder] I can tell you all that the 38th Army Group and the 27th Army Group are simply not at the Nanyuan Airport. [Turns again to look at same spot behind him, over left shoulder.] There is no such place [*sic*]. Rumors like this are total nonsense, designed to fool people.

Military Describes Clearing of the Square

In addition to these problems, I also want to brief you on the operation to clean up Tiananmen Square.

At about 1:30 P.M. on June 4 [1630 GMT June 3], the martial law units arrived in Tiananmen Square to enforce the martial law order and clean up the square. After we arrived, we spent several hours—about three hours or so—repeatedly broadcasting the urgent announcement of the Beijing municipal government and the Headquarters of the Martial Law Units, pointing out that a serious counterrevolutionary rebellion had taken place since the early morning of June 3, and requesting the citizens and students still in the square to leave there as soon as possible. After our repeated broadcast, most of the onlookers and other masses gradually moved out of the square. Only some people still remained around the Monument to the People's Heroes [a Communist monument in Tiananmen Square].

[Zhang continues to read from page before him on table.] We again broadcast the urgent announcement, so that more people could leave the square before the troops formally cleaned up the square. As a result of our repeated broadcasts, some representatives of the student organizations asked our martial law units whether the students could peacefully or voluntarily withdraw from the square. The martial law units promptly accepted their request and, through loudspeakers, again explained to the students that their request had been accepted. [Again looks back, over left shoulder.] In our broadcasts we kept asking the students to leave the square voluntarily and peacefully. Thus, quite a number of students began to leave the square from the southeast exit.

It is quite clear that during the course of withdrawal, not a single person was killed or crushed.

When we began to clean up the square, there were not many people there. When the cleanup began, the troops moved from north to south, moving from the Tiananmen tower toward the monument. As they moved, they left an opening through which the students and the masses in the square could leave voluntarily. After all the students and masses had left, the officers and men of our troops began to examine the tents they left behind to see if there were still people inside. We examined each and every tent. After making sure that there were no more people inside those tents, we used vehicles to knock down those make-shift tents and piled them up into one place. We also knocked down barricades, including things like the so-called goddess statue [the Goddess of Democracy statue which resembled the Statue of Liberty].

[Zhang continues to read from page on table before

him.] During the cleanup process, seven people—some were on a vehicle with tow tanks of gasoline, and some were carrying glass bottles of gasoline—headed by a ringleader from the illegal organization, the Self-Government Union of College Students, attempted to burn and blow up our military vehicles. [Again looks back, over left shoulder.] They also threatened to burn down the Tiananmen Tower. When our cadres and fighters discovered them, they tried to escape with the bottles, heading in the direction of [words indistinct]. We caught them, so they did not achieve their scheme. Thus we can say that the entire cleanup process was basically one of peaceful withdrawal under our powerful and repeated propaganda work.

It is quite clear that during the course of withdrawal, not a single person was killed or crushed. [Zhang again looks over his left shoulder, then smiles. He briefly sits quietly, before suddenly continuing.] . . .

Yuan: Comrade Zhang Gong, please continue.

Civilians Were Violent, Military Restrained

Zhang: One more thing that I would like to say is that, since the imposition of martial law on April 20 [date as heard], all the officers and men of the martial law enforcement troops have exercised maximum restraint vis-à-vis the crowd that encircled the PLA fighters and cadres. Many among the crowd were, certainly, bad elements. For a considerably long period, we adopted the policy of not talking back when abused and not hitting back when hit. Therefore, our troops were pinned down for three nights and days in the area between Gucheng and Bajiao [suburban Beijing streets]. They were unable to have decent meals. They were abused, beaten, and grabbed. Even army commanders and political commissars, encircled and pushed and shoved by the crowd, were forced to stand there for 5 hours. Under these conditions, they exercised great restraint all along. During the period from the night of June 3 to the early morning of June 4—we arrived at Tiananmen at 1:30, as was said just now—we were under the frenzied attacks of the ruffians as we marched toward Tiananmen. You just saw a film. As a matter of fact, we were unable to shoot many of the scenes; there was not enough time for that. . . .

You already saw the end that came to that officer. In addition to that, a soldier was carried to, to . . .

Yuan, interrupting: An overpass.

Zhang: An overpass in Chongwenmen [a suburb of Beijing]. They lifted him and threw him down from the overpass. After killing the soldier by throwing him, they poured gasoline on the body and burned it. They then hoisted the charred body for others to see. We did not record this scene. [Zhang again looks back over his left shoulder.] . . . Many people saw it. In addition to the rather heavy casualties, which Comrade Yuan Mu has already given an account of, our equipment was also greatly damaged. All kinds of military vehicle have been burned. According to preliminary, incomplete figures, hundreds of vehicles have been burned. . . .

At 1:00 this morning, at the interchange in Fuxingmen [suburb of Beijing]—we had set up a checkpoint there to ensure that troop patrols will be able to move around unimpeded and to restore traffic order in the capital—the checkpoint was attacked by two groups of armed ruffians. They attacked the troops with guns [pauses and looks over his left shoulder] . . . guns. Their chieftain is now under arrest. His name is Zhang Jun, twenty-two years of age, a worker at the Chongguang Machinery Plant in Beijing. . . .

Civilian Casualties Could Have Been Larger

These ruffians cannot be more arrogant now. This has been proven by facts. . . . It shows that our troops were overly afraid of hurting the masses and the onlookers, many of whom were agitated and had come to believe the hearsay, and so they always exercised great restraint. If we did not exercise restraint, there simply could not have been that many casualties among us and so much of our equipment destroyed. This is ample proof of facts. There couldn't be so many officers and men who have died or been wounded, nor could there have been so many weapons and equipment destroyed or robbed from them. This is something anyone with some common sense can understand. If the troops, who had weapons in their hands, did not exercise restraint [Zhang smiles], then we would not have needed that many troops and we could have completely . . . [Zhang again looks back over his left shoulder, then changes thought, without finishing the sentence]. The current situation would not have happened. Thus, I think we exercised great restraint.

Our troops did not take actions to defend themselves until the counterrevolutionary rebellion took place on the evening of June 2 and the early morning of June 3. Our self-defense was [words indistinct] something which we took when we could not afford not to. But we still did our best to exercise restraint. This is because our troops are children of the people. Their goal is to serve the people wholeheartedly. In fact, when our cadres and fighters could not distinguish who was a rebel and who was just an ordinary civilian, they simply could not pull the trigger. If they had not exercised restraint, our equipment could not have been destroyed like that. Take a look at our armored vehicles [words indistinct]. The fact that so much equipment has been destroyed and so many cadres and fighters have been beaten up or killed can also account for our troops' restraint. This is all I want to say.

The Thugs Are Still at Work

Yuan Mu: Now I would like to ask Comrade Yuan Liben to report on the losses that Beijing has suffered from the rebellion. . . .

The situation in the capital is still severe since the initial victory was won in our counterattack against the counter-revolutionary rebellion. The thugs have changed their tactics. They have not reconciled themselves to their defeat and are still carrying out furious counterattacks. Their activities generally include the following.

First, they continue spreading rumors to poison the people's minds and incite those people who do not know the facts, and they continue to oppose the government and the people. We have certain difficulties in trying to clarify the truth because of the limited means available to us at the moment. For instance, we were unable to deliver the newspapers yesterday and today.

Yuan Mu: We have not read the newspapers for the past two days.

Yuan Liben, reading from notes without looking up: Therefore, we earnestly hope that the reporters here, for the sake of Beijing's peace and stability as well as the overall interests of the state and the people, will spread the truth to society. Currently, the rumor-mongers are pandering to the tastes of the masses and what they spread is very poisonous. In particular, when the masses' emotions are worked up, it is hard for them to consider problems with a cool head. For instance, a PLA fighter was thrown over the railing of an overpass close to the Chongwen Gate to the street below, where he was burned alive. Even in such a situation, there were still people who were spreading the rumor that the fighter was beaten to death by the masses in anger because he killed three residents. . . .

The rumor-mongers are of course very detestable. But those who spread rumors can always make a rumor sound as if it were 100 percent true. If someone should ask them, "Did you see or just hear it?" they would say that they are not sure. But rumors like that can really poison the people's mind.

Civilians Were Harmed by Thugs, Not Soldiers

Some comrades were indeed brutally murdered. Just now you comrades have seen the video picture. Of course there are other materials and they can all be made public in the future. This is the first point. I believe, as can be seen from the video, the great majority of them were innocent by-standers who went there simply to watch the excitement, not to act against the PLA nor to take part in the riot. Not everyone who appeared in the video is a rioter. In such a chaotic condition where good and bad people were inter-mingled and right and wrong were mixed up, the PLA, dri-ven beyond the limits of forbearance, was forced to take some drastic measures. As a result, some people were acci-dentally killed. To those comrades who were accidentally killed, before I came here, the leading comrade of the State Council told me to express, well, deep regrets. In addition, in the future when it is found out which units or organiza-tions they belong to—some have already been identified. . . .

[Unidentified male voice interrupts from off-camera. Words indistinct.]

Yuan Mu: . . . some have already been identified—the units will be instructed to make satisfactory, appropriate arrangement for their funerals. I hope that the journalistic circles will also relay this attitude of the State Council to everyone.

Of course, there are people who, under the influence of the thugs, did not know the truth and who had misunder-standings of one kind or another about martial law and felt rather sulky about it from the start. When the time came, these people also took to the streets, throwing some stories at the PLA or beating them in some small way. I said that such things could also happen. Therefore, I do not believe that whoever took part in the attack against the PLA are all thugs. I do not see things in this way. I believe that the vast number of students must be separated from the thugs. The bystanders and people who do not know the truth must also be separated from the very few traitors [Yuan Mu immediately correcting], thugs and ruffians. Whom we call thugs and ruffians and those who masterminded the counterrevolutionary rebellion are still those who are described in the letter of the CPC Central Committee and the State Council sent to all party members and the people throughout the country. They are the schemers and organizers behind the scene: people who colluded with overseas hostile forces, people who leaked important, high-level party and state secrets to illegal organizations, and people who conspired and plotted behind the scene. These people did not necessarily go to the streets to do the beating. They might have stayed behind, plotting other things. Strikers, smashers, and looters, those hooligans and gangs, those released from reeducation through labor, and those released from prison after serving their terms without being successfully reformed—these are the people we are talking about, and they include those who came to Beijing from elsewhere to commit crimes.

The Thugs' Numbers Are Small

There is absolutely no intention to indiscriminately call everyone who took to the streets as thugs. I do not recognize this idea. It is also wrong to do so. Precisely in this sense, I said from the very beginning that the current incident is a counterrevolutionary rebellion in nature. The reason it is called a counterrevolutionary rebellion is that there are a very few thugs and ruffians who used extremely cruel, extremely inhuman means against our people's soldiers. I believe that those bystanders, those who generally did not know the truth, could not possibly use that kind of cruel and brutal means against our own troops. They threw the bodies high from the overpass bridge. On top of it, they burned them with gasoline. Their intestines were taken out. Men were beaten to death and the bodies were hung up to show to the public. Men were hit inside the vehicles, and stones were thrown at them even after they were dead. No one could do such a thing unless he harbored deep-seated hatred toward the PLA and the Communist Party. Such people are absolutely very, very few in our country.

Thus, we still have to, first of all, make clear that this rebellion was certainly a counterrevolutionary act, a very serious rebellion. You can see that the methods used were [words indistinct]. Even the personal insult and abuse they heaped against the liberation army were not ordinary abuse. Their cruelty and inhumanity has developed to such an extent. What is more, in just one or two days, more than 500 vehicles were burned, exploded, or destroyed. If a vehicle costs approximately 100,000 yuan, 500 vehicles would cost some 50 million yuan. They had not the least feeling of affection for the state property, the public property. This was absolutely not what the general people could do. They captured ammunition and guns. This was a very clear [distinction?]. Some students in schools have handed over the ammunition and guns of their own accord. One school has handed over more than forty guns. If the students of this school were thugs, how could they have handed over the guns? Certainly not. However, there certainly are some guns still scattered in society. Some people have swaggered around flagrantly, carrying submachine guns, and there have been instances of people shooting people from hiding. I do not mean to say—I do not mean it at all—that all people wounded by mistake were shot from hiding. That would not be seeking truth from facts. However, there were certainly such instances as shooting from hiding. There were certainly the instances where people were shot from hiding and then put the blame on the liberation army. Therefore, the only course for us kindhearted and good people to take is to unite to deal with the very few thugs.

Thus, we still have to, first of all, make clear that this rebellion was certainly a counterrevolutionary act, a very serious rebellion.

We sincerely appeal to all people to understand that, first, this was indeed a shocking counterrevolutionary rebellion, and, second, there are certainly cruel and inhuman thugs in our capital. These thugs are beyond the general imagination of we kindhearted people. Some kind and honest people and some of the masses might not quite understand the fact that the liberation army entered the city to carry out the task of enforcing martial law. We cannot blame these people. Perhaps, there was not enough work of propaganda and explanation, and these people could not understand the theory about this matter and were unclear about the situation. But definitely we cannot view them as thugs. We should isolate the thugs. That is, we should stop the rebellion. We should not be softhearted in dealing with them, but should resolutely strike at them. As for the masses, we should side with them as our people. We should side with the liberation army so as to guarantee that they can carry out the normal task of enforcing martial law. We should neither interfere with them nor upset them nor stir up incidents. If so, I think it will be much easier to stabilize the situation. . . .

Government Will Not Respond to Pressure from Other Countries

Here I also want to make one more point, that is, with regard to current international opinion. [Video shows Yuan Mu gesturing to emphasize.] At present, there are different opinions. It should be said that the current international opinion is not quite uniform with regard to the counterrevolutionary rebellion in China's capital and the struggle to put down the rebellion. There are already people openly condemning us. In addition, there are people who have said that they are not going to give us this or that, that they are going to set this restriction or that, and that they are going to sanction us.

With regard to this point, before I came here I also asked the leading comrade of the State Council [Li Peng] for instruction. He asked me to make two points clear through the media. First, we are not afraid. [Video shows Yuan Mu gesturing to emphasize the point.] No matter what kind of means they use, whether condemnation or sanction, the Chinese people will never permit their intervention in China's internal affairs. Even if we encounter some temporary difficulties as a result of their actions, we must also cope with them. This is because the current struggle to put down the rebellion is one of life-and-death for the party and the state. If you cannot cope with these minor issues, you simply dare not proceed in this way [laughs]. "The State Council and the People's Republic will all be overturned. What is the use of asking for loans or aid from him?" This is the first attitude. [Video shows Yuan Mu appearing defiant.] Second, we also hope to tell, through the media, the international media, foreign statesmen, and the governments that they must not be too short-sighted and that they need to have a somewhat broader point of view. Even though we face difficulties at the present and are in a grim situation and the party and the state can be said to be in a quite critical moment, China's party and government have the ability, methods, and determination to pull through these difficulties. If they approach the problems with a broader point of view, I do not think they will go as far as acting in a way that will solely upset the Chinese government and people, nor do we want to see this happen.

3

Many Reports of the Massacre Were Distorted

Robin Munro

It is no surprise, given the chaos and confusion in and around Tiananmen Square on June 4, 1989, that foreign journalists' accounts of the massacre differed widely. Robin Munro, an American journalist and research associate for the human rights organization Asia Watch, asserts that the Chinese Communist Party took advantage of these conflicting and often inaccurate reports by insisting that their own, equally skewed version of events was the only trustworthy one. Munro, who wrote the following account in 1990, remained in and near the square long after many foreign journalists fled. By interspersing numerous other eyewitness accounts of the massacre with his own, Munro attempts to separate fact from conjecture. For example, he points out that many more common people, the "laobaixing," were killed in the uprising than were students (as many journalists feared) or soldiers (as Communist Party officials maintained). Munro argues that the Chinese government, which prides itself on being an advocate of China's workers, had a much greater fear of a mass uprising of dissatisfied laborers than of student protests. Munro also reveals that, contrary to the government's claim that the People's Liberation Army was subject to wholesale slaughter by protesters, in numerous cases, soldiers were sympathetic with the movement and peacefully gave up their vehicles and weapons to the protesters.

Excerpted from "Who Died in Beijing, and Why," by Robin Munro, *Nation*, June 11, 1990. Copyright © 1990 by The Nation Company, Inc. Reprinted with permission.

Among the revolts that ignited the Communist world in 1989, China's was the great failure. On the night of June 3–4 the Chinese Communist Party showed the world that it would stop at nothing to maintain its monopoly of power.

But what exactly did happen that night? Few modern events have been covered as intensively by the Western news media as the Tiananmen Square democracy movement. Yet in crucial respects the denouement remains shrouded in myth. In the immediate aftermath, some basic notions took hold: Journalists spoke routinely of the slaughter of students, of "the massacre in Tiananmen Square." A year later [1990], that phrase has become the official shorthand for what happened in Beijing.

A revisionist trend currently emerging in some Western circles maintains that there was no massacre. That is preposterous. A massacre did take place—but not in Tiananmen Square, and not predominantly of students. The great majority of those who died (perhaps as many as a thousand in all) were workers, or *laobaixing* ("common folk," or "old hundred names"), and they died mainly on the approach roads in western Beijing. Several dozen people died in the immediate environs of the square and a few in the square itself. But to speak of that as the real massacre distorts the city wide nature of the carnage and diminishes the real political drama that unfolded in Tiananmen Square.

Western Journalists Report from the Square

Hundreds of reporters were in Beijing that night, but very few were present for the climactic clearing of the square by the army. Many were on the real killing grounds of western Beijing, along Chang'an Boulevard and Fuxingmen Boulevard, and reported vividly and accurately on what they saw. Some had been arrested, and others were pinned down behind roadblocks. Others still were back in their hotels for early-morning filing deadlines. Most who were in the vicinity of the square when the army arrived, however, left quickly and out of legitimate fear for their safety. . . .

Sorting Fact from Fiction

Some people do accept that the bulk of the killing took place outside Tiananmen Square. [Ted] Koppel, for example, in his June 29 special, noted the distinction but downplayed it as a "loophole" to be exploited by the Chinese government.

But insisting on factual precision is not just a matter of splitting hairs. For the geography of the killing reveals much about the government's cold political logic and its choice of targets—as well as the likely scenario of the next round of pro-democracy struggles in China. The regime squandered its remaining popular legitimacy in a single night of bloodshed, and unless it can somehow learn the art of compromise, the fact that a sizable section of "the masses" was ready to fight back, together with the potential unreliability of the army, provides the ingredients for a possible replay of a . . . [military] revolt.

> *Hundreds of reporters were in Beijing that night, but very few were present for the climactic clearing of the square by the army.*

Journalism may be only the rough draft of history, but if left uncollected it can forever distort the future course of events. Nothing serves the cause of China's students and laobaixing better than the unvarnished truth, for it speaks eloquently of their heroism and of the regime's cowardice and brutality. But Western criticisms based on a false version of the clearing of Tiananmen Square have handed the butchers of Beijing needless propaganda victories in the U.N. and elsewhere. They have also distracted attention from the main target of the continuing repression: the mass movement that eventually superseded the students' protest actions. The credit for inspiring the movement and upholding the banner of nonviolence will always belong to the students. But only by refocusing attention on the laobaixing will we understand why China, a year later, continues to be ruled by the jackboot, the rifle and the thought police. . . .

Chinese political tradition has long conferred a limited degree of tolerance and immunity on students, a certain latitude of action not shared by other groups—and especially not by the workers. This relative privilege was enhanced during the decade of reform in the 1980s, as Deng Ziaoping moved rapidly toward a historic compromise with the intelligentsia (whom Mao Zedong had ruthlessly persecuted) in order to advance China's modernization program and facilitate the economic opening to the West. This official stance was fraught with problems, of course, since greater freedom for the students and intellectuals inevitably brought with it the danger of corrosive bourgeois liberal ideas from the West.

Laobaixing Are the Real Threat to Government

But that was nothing compared with the other danger that had preoccupied the party since the start of the reform process. This was the prospect of organized unrest and dissent among the urban working class. . . . Above all, it was the rapid trend toward just such a movement . . . in Beijing and other major cities last spring [1989] that determined the uncompromising character of the crackdown when it finally came. The students had initiated the movement and brilliantly outmaneuvered the government but with the intervention of broader social forces on Tiananmen Square, the students soon lost control of the situation and their leadership became chronically divided. . . .

This specter of emerging cross-class solidarity led directly to the authorities' decision to impose martial law in Beijing on May 20. But again, the strength of the popular response caught China's leaders unawares: The tanks and troop columns were halted at all major points of entry to the city by a human wall of peaceful protesters, and after a few days the soldiers were forced to withdraw to their barracks in the suburbs. Action groups formed spontaneously throughout Beijing. These included "dare-to-die squads" of workers and other laobaixing, who vowed to die rather than let the army into the city; the workers' pickets, who, together with formidably organized contingents of student pickets, patrolled the neighborhoods and maintained order (the public security forces and traffic police were nowhere to be seen after May 20); and the "little flying tigers," large groups of youths on motorcycles who sped around the city on liaison missions for the movement. The laobaixing were now in a posture of peaceful, nonviolent but direct confrontation with the government and army, and similar "turmoil"—to use the party's term—rapidly emerged in dozens of other cities.

Students Draw Support

Moreover, the laobaixing were beginning to articulate their own grievances. These were mostly a product of the decade-long economic reforms, which, though broadly popular, had also generated a range of serious social tensions: sharp income polarization, spiraling commodity prices, an acute shortage of acceptable housing and—last but by no means least—rampant corruption, speculation and profiteering by government and party officials. The authorities probably overestimated the political challenge that these new workers' and citizens' groups posed. The groups were spontaneous, and while their visible impact and propaganda effect were considerable, they lacked any distinct ideological framework or program. But the party's alarm was real. . . .

In the spirit of [Deng Xiaoping's] April 26 editorial, the students and intellectuals would, by and large, be spared. The laobaixing, on the other hand, would be mercilessly punished in order to eradicate organized popular unrest for a generation. The arenas of conflict on the night of June 3–4 overlapped, but they were essentially separate. The real killing grounds, the theater of the popular uprising and massacre, lay mainly on the periphery, above all along western Chang'an Boulevard and out to the western suburbs. Here, the laobaixing fought and died to defend the center: Tiananmen Square. The prodemocracy movement stayed firm in its commitment to the principles of dialogue and nonviolence, and it resorted to force on that final night only out of desperation and rage. Once the army had embarked on the rape of Beijing it was clear that all was lost. In the eye of the storm, around the Monument to the People's Heroes, stood the students brave, resolute but ultimately protected within a charmed circle. At the last minute, in the square itself, with its most lethal resources arrayed against the moral authority of youth, the government stepped back from the brink of a slaughter of incalculable proportions.

The Bloody Road to Tiananmen

There were more than 1,000 foreign journalists in Beijing on the night of the army's final drive to clear Tiananmen Square, and many of them followed the advance of the main People's Liberation Army (P.L.A.) assault force through the western suburbs as it plowed murderously through the crowds of laobaixing that formed at all points to block its path. Most of the foreign film footage of the massacre was shot in this sector of the city, in neighborhoods like Muxidi, Fuxingmen and Liubukou, where hundreds of unarmed protesters and innocent bystanders were mowed down by random gunfire from semiautomatic weapons. The troops apparently made no distinction between these people and the small number who hurled stones, rocks and Molotov cocktails or set fire to vehicles that had been used as roadblocks. Since this main theater of the massacre was by and large well covered by the foreign news media, we will focus here on some lesser-known aspects of the action along western Chang'an and Fuxingmen—subsequently dubbed "Blood Boulevard" by the people of Beijing.

As far as is known, the first violence came at around 10:30 P.M. on June 3 at Gongzhufen, some two miles west of Muxidi, where vanguard contingents of the assault force used about twenty armored personnel carriers (A.P.C.) to crash through bus barricades that were blocking the circular intersection. A West German student living in Beijing at the time witnessed the incident and reports that many people were crushed to death as the A.P.C.s went through and soldiers fired indiscriminately at the crowd. A Finnish journalist who was also standing nearby reports seeing two soldiers with AK-47 assault rifles suddenly descend from the tenth truck of a convoy of fifty or so that drove through the gaps in the barricades. "They were torn to pieces by the crowd," she says. "It was a horrible sight." The pattern of the night's conflict, then, was set from the start: Random and brutal killings by the army came first, followed swiftly by a small number of revenge killings of troops by distraught, and increasingly insurgent, citizens. . . .

Army Not as Dedicated as Party Wanted

China may have come closer to a . . . military revolt than is generally recognized. According to a report in the *South China Morning Post* on December 28, P.L.A. Chief Political Commissary Yang Baibing revealed in a confidential speech earlier that month that 21 officers and cadres with ranks of divisional commander or above, 36 officers with ranks of regimental or battalion commander, and 54 officers with the rank of company chief breached discipline in a serious manner during the struggle to crush the "counterrevolutionary rebellion" in June. In addition, 1,400 soldiers "shed their weapons and ran away."

In the days that followed the massacre, the Chinese authorities repeatedly televised an astonishing piece of footage that showed dozens of A.P.C.s being torched by the crowd in the vicinity of the Military Museum, just west of Muxidi. The commentary said that many of the occupants had preferred to be burned alive rather than open fire on their compatriots; it also clearly implied that this had occurred in the early evening of June 3, before nightfall. This footage was a cornerstone of the government's "Big Lie," evidence of the "counterrevolutionary rebellion" that had obliged the government to respond with force.

In the spirit of [Deng Xiaoping's] April 26 editorial, the students and intellectuals would, by and large, be spared.

The reality was very different. At about 9 A.M. on Sunday, June 4, several foreign witnesses, inspecting the devastation of the previous night, were stunned to see a column of some three dozen A.P.C.s suddenly appear from the west and come to a halt at the Muxidi intersection. The first vehicle had struck the remnants of a barricade; a second had run into its rear, bringing the convoy to a halt. A large crowd materialized from the neighboring alleyways and surrounded the now silent armored column. The first troops to emerge were beaten, and at least one is thought to have been killed. Only the intervention of student pickets, who negotiated safe passage for the troops, headed off a pitched battle and, perhaps, a fresh round of killing. Several hundred soldiers simply walked away, leaving behind their lethal hardware for the crowd to muse over. Within half an hour, all the A.P.C.s had been set on fire, and a towering column of black smoke could be seen for miles. It may be no coincidence that this incident took place right outside the main offices of Central Chinese Television, from whose rooftop the scene was exhaustively videotaped. But a more significant explanation is that the troops actually deserted. A prominent West German Sinologist who was present described seeing soldiers escorted away from their vehicles. One A.P.C., he says, "opened the top lids, and a hand appeared waving a white piece of cloth. Soldiers emerged and gave their automatic rifles to the young men receiving them. They hugged.". . .

Tiananmen Square is the largest public space in the world. It extends over 100 acres, and no single eyewitness could hope to encompass the complex and confusing sequence of events that unfolded there on the night of June 3–4. My own account, therefore, is supplemented by the testimony of others who saw what happened at crucial moments.

Clearing of the Square Begins

I arrived at the square at about 1:15 A.M. Large crowds were fleeing eastward along Chang'an Boulevard. Continuous gunfire sounded from the northwest sector of the square, and a crippled A.P.C. lay blazing in the northeast corner, set afire by Molotov cocktails. Its tracks had been jammed with steel bars and traffic dividers. A CNN film unit and a number of British journalists were on the scene. According to John Simpson of the BBC, three A.P.C. crew members had been beaten to death and a fourth escorted to safety by student pickets. Jonathan Mirsky of the *London Observer*, who was beaten by armed policemen with truncheons [batons] just before I arrived, says he saw several people shot dead near the huge portrait of Mao on Tiananmen Gate.

Looking over to the northwest corner of the square, I saw with horror that the tents of the Beijing Workers' Autonomous Federation were in flames, and I ran over to see if any of my friends from the federation were dead or wounded. Twenty yards away, a menacing group of about 200 heavily armed troops stood facing the tents. This was the advance party of the main invasion force of the P.L.A., which would arrive at the square at around 2 A.M. after smashing its way along western Chang'an. By now the crowds had fled from this area. Only the figure of a young man was visible, wandering slowly around the burning tents and gathering up piles of documents, which he implored me to take to the students on the Monument to the People's Heroes. This I did.

Nearly all the students had withdrawn by now to the three tiers of the monument: 3,000 to 5,000 of them perhaps, huddled tightly together. Their makeshift tent encampment, which sprawled over an area of several hundred square yards to the north of the monument, was virtually deserted. The students seemed calm, almost resigned. There was no panic, though the stutter of gunfire could be heard on the fringes of the square and beyond. Abruptly the government loudspeakers boomed into life with an endlessly repeated message: Everyone was to leave the square immediately; a "serious counterrevolutionary rebellion" had broken out and the martial-law troops were empowered to clear Tiananmen Square by any means necessary. . . .

Another witness to the clashes in the south was the renowned writer Lao Gui. At about 1:30 he wrote, "There was a continuous sound of gunfire coming from Zhushikou [about half a mile south of the square]. Red flares were going up all around. I met a Western reporter at the cypress trees by the Mao Memorial Hall who told me, 'I saw three people killed with my own eyes, their stomachs were blown open, down at Zhushikou.' Other accounts suggest that at least several dozen people were killed by troops as the army forced its way up through the southern neighborhoods. Close to 2:00 a force of about a hundred troops tried to enter the square from the southwest corner. 'Suddenly there was intense firing and bullets flying all over the place,' says NBC cameraman Tony Wasserman, who was there. 'And somewhere along the way someone gets it in the stomach and someone in the ankle. Before this, the crowd grabs some soldiers from the southwest corner again and they beat the . . . out of them.' A little later, according to CBS cameraman Derek Williams, 'In came the paratroopers. . . . They were real . . . kickers.'". . .

Few Protesters Remain in the Square

After the arrival of the main force [in the square], only a sprinkling of people—apparently not students but ordinary residents and workers—remained in the northern part of the square, between Chang'an and the monument. The statue of democracy looked more dramatic than ever, facing Mao's portrait and the troops beneath it through the flames and smoke that still billowed from the crippled A.P.C. At around 2:15, there was a terrific burst of AK-47 fire, lasting several minutes, from the vicinity of Tiananmen Gate. I hit the deck. Most of the crowd fled southward, toward the monument, but I saw no one injured. At more or less the same moment, just a few hundred yards away, several hundred troops moved across from Tiananmen Gate to seal off the northeast entrance to the square, blocking off eastern Chang'an Boulevard to the north of the History Museum. A student named Ke Feng, one of the main organizers of the statue of democracy project, was hiding in a small park nearby. In the first five minutes or so, he saw about twenty people in the vicinity of the pedestrian underpass hit by "stray bullets," including "five people who fell and couldn't get up again." Some 500 troops emerged from behind the History Museum, although these did not appear to be carrying rifles. As another 200 to 300 advanced from the direction of Tiananmen Gate, the crowd began shouting, "Fascists!" and "General Strike!"; others sang the "Internationale" [Chinese national anthem]. Ke Feng, still hiding nearby, tells of the soldiers jumping for joy, as if playing a game. . . . An officer kept shouting through a megaphone for about fifteen minutes, "Leave immediately, we'll shoot to kill!" in an extraordinary, suicidal act of defiance, someone drove an articulated twin-carriage bus at full speed straight at the soldiers. In the words of Kenneth Qiang, a council member of the Hong Kong Student Federation, "The driver was dragged out by soldiers and clubbed to the ground with their rifle butts. The crowd was incensed, and they ran forward to within fifty meters of the troops, throwing glass bottles at them. I heard two separate gunshots. The driver fell to the ground dead. . . ."

By 3:00 I could see no other foreigners anywhere in the square. The foreign television crews had apparently evacuated the place. "I now feel guilty about the decision," the BBC's Simpson wrote later in *Granta* [British literary magazine]. "It was wrong: we ought to have stayed in the square, even though the other camera crews had already left and it might have cost us our lives." Simpson's decision, as we shall see, had a crucial impact on his reporting during the rest of the night. . . .

Remaining Students Hold Firm

Abruptly, on the stroke of 4:00, all the lights in Tiananmen Square went out. Back at the southeast corner of the monument, we [he and American journalist Richard Nations] waited anxiously, but the assault did not come. The students remained seated on the monument, just as before. No one made any move to leave. Noiselessly, as if in a dream, two busloads of student reinforcements appeared in the square from the southeast, coming to a halt yards from where we stood. The student loudspeakers crackled back to life and a voice announced—deadpan, as if reading a railroad schedule—"we will now play the 'Internationale,' to raise our fighting spirit." I wondered what the soldiers were feeling, out there in the dark. Were the students counting on the embarrassment factor to save them if all else failed? But still the attack did not materialize. When some people set fire to the abandoned tents and piles of garbage to the west of the monument—perhaps so the assault would not take place in darkness—the student leadership rebuked them: "Keep order, stay calm. We must create no pretext whatsoever for them." At about 4:15 [A.M.] an array of lights, like fairy lights on a Christmas tree, suddenly came on all across the front of the Great Hall of the People, filling the west side of the square with a soft, luminous glow. At the same time, floodlights went on along the facade of the Forbidden City. Next, the southernmost doors of the Great Hall swung open, disgorging a human river of gun-toting troops, many with fixed bayonets. According to CBS's Derek Williams, who was close by, "They came around and joined a large blocking force which stretched in an L-shape down the west side of the street and then cut across the square in front of the Mao Mausoleum." Troops now began firing at the monument from the History Museum steps, and we could see the sparks flying from the obelisk, high above head level.

Tiananmen Square is the largest public space in the world.

It was now just after 4:30. The square was empty of people, and scattered with the forlorn debris of the abandoned encampment. The 3,000 or so students remained huddled on the steps and the three levels of the monument. Again, the student loudspeakers crackled to life, and someone who announced himself as a leader of the Beijing Students' Autonomous Federation took the microphone: "Students! We must on no account quit the square. We will now pay the highest price possible for the sake of securing democracy in China. Our blood shall be the consecration." My heart sank. After a few minutes, someone else spoke, this time a leader of the Beijing Workers' Autonomous Federation: "We must all leave here immediately, for a terrible bloodbath is about to take place. There are troops surrounding us on all sides and the situation is now extraordinarily dangerous. To wish to die here is no more than an immature fantasy." A lengthy silence ensued. Then Hou Dejian spoke. (Hou, a Taiwan-born popular singer, was one of four people who had begun a hunger strike on the monument on June 2.) "We have won a great victory," he said. "But now we must leave this place. We have shed too much of our blood. We cannot afford to lose any more. . . . We four hunger strikers will remain on the monument until everyone else has left safely, and then we too will leave. . . ."

The question of what happened next has probably been the single biggest point of controversy in the reporting of the events of June 3–4 in Beijing. Correspondent Richard Roth of CBS had time to file one last report before soldiers arrested him and took him into the Great Hall of the People. Soldiers have spotted CBS News cameraman Derek Williams and myself and are angrily dragging us away. And a moment later it begins: "powerful bursts of automatic weapons, raging gunfire for a minute and a half that lasts as long as a nightmare. And we see no more." The film was confiscated. Roth's dramatic commentary, aired on the June 4 *CBS Evening News* and accompanied by footage shot two hours earlier, left the clear impression that troops had opened fire on the students as they evacuated the monument. . . .

What Nations and I saw, from our position twenty-five yards southeast of the monument, was unforgettable. For an agonizing minute, it seemed as if the students might not comply with the decision to leave. Then, slowly, they began to stand up and descend from the monument. As the first group filed past us, heading toward the open southeast corner of the square, we burst into spontaneous applause. Many in the ten-deep column, each contingent following the banners of its college, had tears rolling down their cheeks. All looked shaken; many were trembling or unsteady on their feet. But all looked proud and unbeaten. One group shouted, "Down with the Communist Party!" The first time I had ever heard this openly said in China. . . .

Journalists Are Feared Dead

But according to a widely reprinted "eyewitness" account, which first ran in a Hong Kong paper and was purportedly written by a student from Beijing's Qinghua University, nearly all of us had already been killed, mowed down at point-blank range by a bank of a dozen machine guns just after 4:00. The survivors were then either chased across the square by tanks and crushed or else beaten to death with clubs. This story was picked up by, among others, *The New York Times* (although reporter Nicholas Kristof quickly challenged it), *The Washington Post* and *The San Francisco Examiner*. In terms of lurid invention, it was in a class of its own. Astonishingly, however, it is only one of several such accounts, most of which say the mass slayings took place just before 5:00. Wuer Kaixi, one of the principal student leaders, said he had seen "about 200 students" cut down by gunfire in the predawn assault. But he was not there: He had been driven to safety in a van several hours earlier. How could these fabrications have gained so much acceptance?

The question of what happened next has probably been the single biggest point of controversy in the reporting of the events of June 3–4 in Beijing.

There were, by my count, ten Western journalists in the vicinity of the monument at the time in question, as well as a handful of diplomats and Hong Kong Chinese. At least two of the reporters—Claudia Rosett of *The Asian Wall Street Journal* and John Pomfret of the *Associated Press*—filed accurate accounts of the evacuation, but these were isolated paragraphs buried in long reports from other parts of the city. With Roth and Williams of CBS under arrest in the Great Hall of the People, not to emerge until 5:30, the only foreign film footage of the evacuation is that taken by the Spanish TV crew, who insist they saw no killing. In an interesting footnote, their reporter, Juan Restrepo, who was separated from his crew all night, says that their film of the night's events was garbled by his editors at *Television Española* in Madrid, creating the false impression that killings had taken place during the evacuation of the square.

Of all the comments by TV reporters who left the square, perhaps the most telling are those of John Simpson, whose BBC news team won a raft of awards for its coverage of events in Beijing. Simpson, as we saw, felt remorseful about leaving. But his account for *Granta* reveals how the sense of impending disaster that led the news media to abandon the square also predisposed them to believe that the worst then actually happened: "Someone should have been there when the massacre took place, filming what happened, showing the courage of the students as they were surrounded by tanks and the army advancing, firing as it went." As dawn drew near on June 4, from a safe but very incomplete vantage point half a mile away on an upper floor of the Beijing Hotel (from which the Monument to the People's Heroes is completely hidden from view), Simpson wrote, "We filmed the tanks as they drove over the tents. . . . Dozens of people seem to have died in that way, and those who saw it said they could hear the screams of the people inside the tents over the noise of the tanks. We filmed as the lights in the square were switched off at four A.M. They were switched on again forty minutes later, when the troops and the tanks moved toward the Monument itself, shooting first in the air and then, again, directly at the students themselves, so that the steps of the Monument and the heroic reliefs which decorated it were smashed by bullets."

Remaining Journalists Witness Final Clearing

As Simpson's crew was filming, Japanese photo journalist Imaeda Koichi was in the northern part of the square. Koichi reports seeing no killing there, although he also says, "I did see some students in the tents, not many, only in three of the tents." Restrepo of *Television Espanola* had earlier checked all the tents in the vicinity of the Goddess of Democracy and says, "I can assure you that there were not more than five people inside the tents at around 3 A.M. . . ."

Lingering doubts about a small group of students who may have remained on the top level of the monument are dispelled by a recent remarkable eyewitness account by Yu Shuo, a former professor at People's University who now lives in exile in Paris. "As I was talking to [an army] officer," she says, "I suddenly realized that I was the last person left at the monument. As I walked down the terrace, I saw a line of characters on the relief: 'On June 4, 1989, the Chinese people shed their blood and died for democracy.' As I turned around, I saw that a soldier was about to pierce a bed with his bayonet. I saw two feet sticking out from it. . . . I rushed forward and dragged the feet. A boy fell down from the bed; he was not completely awake yet. He was the last student to leave the square. . . ."

By now it was broad daylight; the evacuation was complete. At the southern end of the square, Nations and I witnessed one final skirmish between stone throwers and soldiers who opened fire before running off with the crowd on their heels. We finally decided it was time to get the hell out. As far as we can ascertain, we were the last foreigners to leave Tiananmen Square. It was 6:15. . . .

Chinese Government Manipulated the Facts

To conclude, we should turn to two Chinese activists from last year's [1989] democracy movement, both of whom witnessed the final clearing of the square, for an answer to the question posed at the outset: Why does it matter where the massacre took place? Kong Jiesheng, a famous novelist and essayist, says: "Now, when the power-holding clique in Beijing is still unrepentant about the June 4 massacre but also sorely vexed by the criticisms and sanctions imposed by numerous countries, rebukes from outside China based on ill-founded concepts have given those vicious thugs precisely the 'spiritual shield' they so desperately need. It makes plausible their lengthy refutations of outside criticisms as being mere 'stuff and nonsense' and much ado about nothing"— the very phrase used by General Secretary Jiang Zemin when asked by Barbara Walters, on ABC's *20/20* on May 18, about "the massacre in Tiananmen Square."

But Lao Gui should have the last word: "Because of hatred of the murderer, one sometimes cannot resist exaggerating the severity of the crime. This is understandable. . . . But those butchers then take advantage of this opportunity 'to clarify the truth,' using one truth to cover up ten falsehoods. They exploit the fact that no one died during the clearing of Tiananmen Square to conceal the truth that some deaths and injuries did occur there earlier. And they use the fact that there was no bloodbath in Tiananmen Square to cover up the truth about the bloodbaths in Muxidi, Nanchizi and Liubukou. Why do we give them such an opportunity?"

4

Survivors Describe Their Ordeal

Tom Fennell

Many civilians in the streets of Beijing on June 4, 1989, could tell their own tales of fear and bloodshed. In 1999, *Maclean's* reporter Tom Fennell interviewed two such civilians, a husband and wife who now live in Canada and who personally witnessed the killing of their fellow citizens. They, like many of their activist peers living both inside and outside of China, are pessimistic their home country will ever be ruled by a democratic government.

Sheng Xue separates out two large colour photographs of a baby-faced Beijing schoolgirl named Zhang Jin. "It's so sad," Sheng murmurs as she tenderly places the pictures of Jin on the dining room table in her small apartment in suburban Toronto. In one, 19-year-old Jin leans smiling against a taxi, bundled against the first cold days of autumn in a heavy red sweater and long black scarf. In the other, Jin's chubby face is ashen, her brown eyes closed forever beneath the ragged red hole that a soldier's bullet left in the middle of her forehead. "Jin," says Sheng, folding her arms across her chest and gazing at the picture of her fellow protester, "died in my husband's arms."

Jin, like thousands of students, workers and academics who faced the People's Liberation Army in Beijing's Tiananmen Square on June 4, 1989, had been swept up in the pro-democracy movement that transformed the capital that spring. The demonstrators wanted freedom, but after nearly 50 days of mounting protests that threatened to spread beyond Beijing, the country's hardline leaders responded with tanks and guns—and left up to 3,000 people dead. Sheng (her surname) and her husband, Dong Xin, stood with the students during the bloody massacre. And last week [June 4, 1999], as Chinese police kept the square sealed off and continued their crackdown on pro-democracy dissidents, the couple prepared to join thousands of people around the world in a candlelight vigil marking the 10th anniversary of the uprising. "Tiananmen was the last chance for democracy," Sheng said as she prepared a meal of shrimp, fried oysters and fish in her apartment. "We never had it before and we will never have it again."

Sheng, 36, is now the Canadian correspondent for Radio Free Asia, a U.S.-funded network broadcasting into China. Husband Dong, 42, works as an electronics technician. They met while working on a film in Beijing extolling the virtues of China's one-child policy. The two became fiercely opposed to the Communist leadership, yet their political backgrounds could hardly have been more different. In fact, the paths that led the couple to the square in 1989 intertwine with the history of China itself.

Dong's father had embraced communism from the start, joining Mao Tse-tung's revolutionary army when he was just 13. He eventually became a senior police officer in Beijing and constantly reminded his son of Mao's maxim that all good flowed from the state. Sheng's father, by contrast, was an academic who was branded a spy when the Communists came to power in 1949. To "purify" him, he was forced into nearly 20 years of manual labour. Though just children, Sheng and her sister were branded subversives and beaten up by their fellow students. "I grew up knowing there was something very wrong with Chinese society," said Sheng.

Peaceful Protest Turns Violent

Even so, her cynicism seemed to melt away in the spring of 1989. The whole city, she recalled, appeared to be caught up in the spirit of reform. Demonstrators danced to the music of rock bands and students kissed in the sunshine. Nothing seemed impossible. Strangers would suddenly engage in political debate and even a gang of humorous thieves in Sheng's neighbourhood put up posters saying they were going on "strike," and went off to join the festivities in the square. "It was," said Sheng, "something quite amazing."

But the Communist leadership, dominated by an increasingly angry Deng Xiaoping, had mobilized the army in Beijing's suburbs. On June 3, as Sheng was eating dinner with her family, troops began streaming by her home near the square. "I ran to the window and saw the army was in the city," she recalled. "I started to cry." She rushed into the street where she found hundreds of people fighting to stop the soldiers' advance. "We picked up stones and threw them at the tanks," said Sheng, "but what can you do? You can't block it."

She rushed into the street where she found hundreds of people fighting to stop the soldiers' advance.

She returned home at 3 A.M. on June 4, but a few hours later she went back into the street and for the first time realized the full extent of the violence. "On my way to the square I met people carrying bodies," said Sheng. "I could see in their eyes that they were very, very angry."

Sheng's husband, who worked in a store near the square, watched more than 20 people die, including one man who stood on the front bumper of a troop truck and was gunned down. Others played a sometimes deadly game of chicken with the troops. "We would yell 'Nazi fascist,'" said Sheng, "and then they would fire at us."

The doomed teenager, Zhang Jin, had also come down to the square. "She was standing in front of our store when we heard gunfire," said Dong. "She fell and we opened the door and carried her to the backyard." Jin was still breathing but would soon die. "She had a friend with her," recalled Dong. "He was upset and grabbed a knife and wanted to go out and fight with the soldiers." Angry, Dong returned to the front of the store where hair, bone and blood from Jin's head was still stuck to the door. "I stood there," he said, "and told the people going by what had happened here."

Dissidents Still Under Pressure

The number of people killed in the streets near the square and beyond is still uncounted; some activists suggest 1,000, while foreign diplomats have put it at around 3,000. Close to 3,000 were also arrested. The most prominent student leaders, including female firebrand Chai Ling and cerebral theorist Wang Dan, who addressed a rally in Toronto last week [June 4, 1999], have been released and are living abroad, mostly in the United States.

Amnesty International [a human rights organization], however, says as many as 2,000 dissidents remain in prison, including hundreds—241 are documented—from Tiananmen. Sheng, who came to Canada in 1990 on a student visa, says she is deeply worried about them, and produces four large sheets of paper she says were stolen from a Beijing prison. Down the sides are printed the names of the jailed protesters, and their purported crimes. "Life for setting a fire," said Sheng, pointing to one of the names. "Fifteen years for robbery," she said of another. There are also reports that dissidents were executed in the period after the crackdown.

China has never allowed public protests to take place on the June 4 anniversary. This year [1999], the square remains blocked off, ostensibly to prepare for the 50th anniversary celebration of the founding of the People's Republic on Oct. 1, 1949. The crackdown on dissidents has never stopped. The fledgling China Democracy Party was hit hard earlier this year when three top leaders got lengthy jail sentences. Several Tiananmen veterans were picked up in May.

Hopes for Democracy Are Fading

But despite lingering memories of the 1989 carnage, most Chinese now seem much more focused on the booming economy than on politics. As a businessman named Chen put it to *Maclean's* as he passed Tiananmen Square last week [June 4, 1999]: "The students today are only interested in earning money and getting ahead." Or joining the occasional authorized protest. In early May, the government carefully orchestrated demonstrations by students angered by the U.S. bombing of China's embassy in Belgrade [which the U.S. government claims was an accident]. Many analysts saw the rallies as an opportunity to take steam out of the looming Tiananmen anniversary.

Ren Wanding, one of the few major dissidents who is still free in China, told *Maclean's* it could take generations before democracy comes to China. "But everything," he said, "starts from a small basis and by small groups of people." Canada's Sheng is far more pessimistic. "The Chinese government is very tough," she said. "It's over."

Chapter 3

The Legacy of Tiananmen

1

The Student Movement Was Self-Defeating

Liu Binyan

In the years since the Tiananmen Square Massacre, exiled Chinese journalist Liu Binyan's views of the event have changed dramatically. Soundly behind the student protesters shortly after the crackdown, Binyan recanted that position a decade later, saying that their approach to the protests was flawed in many ways. Binyan now maintains that the students, instead of attempting to overthrow the Communist regime, should have set smaller, more realistic goals for their protest. He maintains that had they negotiated with reform-friendly government officials such as Zhao Ziyang and left the Square when it became apparent that the government would not yield to their pressure, lives could have been spared and the democratic movement could have gained incremental, yet crucial ground.

Today, China's political climate is much different than it was in 1989. Many people have benefited from economic reforms put in place since the massacre, so they have fewer incentives to support calls for political reform. In the following interview, Binyan advises China's new generation of student reformists to reach out to China's huge population of workers and peasants as potential allies, instead of making the same mistake the students did in 1989 by dismissing them as unimportant to their cause. If they do so, Binyan predicts they have a chance at uniting the country under a banner of reform.

Human Rights Watch: What impact if any, do you think the student movement had on changes that have taken place in

From Liu Binyan's interview, www.hrw.org, June 1999. Copyright © 1999 by Human Rights Watch. Reprinted with permission.

China up to now on issues ranging from, for example, personal freedoms, openness of the political system, and tolerance for dissent?

Liu Binyan: One of the important reasons for the Tiananmen Movement's failure is that at the peak of the movement, both the students and the government had some illusions. The government felt for the first time ever as if it were on the verge of being toppled; the student leaders thought once the government sent troops to the Square, the whole nation would rise up to their call, thus leading to the collapses of the government.

But neither of these two illusions were true. The massacre and the ensuing large-scale arrests and purging resulted in the annihilation of the democratic forces, and the fruits achieved through the years of struggle to gain freedom in some fields were all gone.

Economic Improvements Passify Many

Deng Xiaoping's tactics of buying social stability with money succeeded; the collapse of the Soviet Union and East European countries, which had encouraged the Chinese people to struggle for democracy, began to have a negative effect in the nineties. Some Chinese even thought that the failure of the Tiananmen Movement had prevented the chaos that was happening in these other countries.

The personal freedom enjoyed by the Chinese people had undergone considerable expansion in the nineties. This was the result of the spontaneous changes that happened during the process of economic reform. It was also the result of the efforts of the Communist Party to divert people's concerns from politics.

One positive effect of the Tiananmen Movement is that it made the Chinese people realize their own political potential. We also need to draw lessons from its failure.

Students' Rigidity Leads to Failure

Thinking about it now, do you think what the students, and later the workers and others, were asking the government to do was what they should have been asking? What would you have asked?

The cause for the failure of the Movement was that the participants did not fully understand the true situation in China nor its history since the founding of the People's Republic. If I had gone back to China in 1989, I would have told the students that democracy could not be obtained in one movement, and that only limited goals could be achieved. I would have tried to persuade the students to use correct strategies and tactics, to negotiate with the government in mid-May, and to withdraw from the Square, though it is unpredictable whether I would have been able to convince them.

What do you think of the strategies and tactics the students, workers, and others employed? Looking back, do you think they were appropriate? With the advantage of hindsight, how would you change them?

The greatest mistake of the students was that they refused any compromise. They did not know the necessity of cooperating with the reformist forces within the Party, thus making all Zhao Ziyang's efforts fail so that Zhao had to resign. Their contempt for the workers and peasants was shocking. They almost never made efforts to win over the workers but on the contrary refused their participation. In mid-May they turned over two teachers from Hunan province who splashed ink on Mao's portrait to the police to show that they were not radicals. These two facts show that their own safety was their first priority. If we look at the power struggles in the Square and their performance in exile, we will realize that many of the leaders are too self-centered.

One of the important reasons for the Tiananmen Movement's failure is that at the peak of the movement, both the students and the government had some illusions.

What part do you think intellectuals played in the movement? What part do you think they should have played?

The intellectuals should assume the chief responsibility. Since the eighties, intellectuals have put too much emphasis on their own work and study and distanced themselves further and further from the reality of society. They did not impart knowledge about history and reality to the young students. At the same time, the lack of commitment and the lack of premonition about possible eruption of social crises made them totally unprepared for the coming turmoil. Therefore, they could not provide much needed ideas, theory, strategy, and tactics to the masses.

Based on your experiences from 1989 until now, if you could ask one thing of the current government in China, what would it be?

I would want to tell the government to judge the hour and size up the situation. If they don't want China to be bogged down in chaos, they should allow freedom of association as ensured by the constitution, and let the exiles return to the country. The Communist Party must first guarantee democracy within the Party.

Binyan Advises New Reformists

If you were advising Chinese students today on how to bring about support for human rights improvements and democratic change, what would you tell them?

I want to tell them that they must be highly vigilant toward the new conservative forces—the nouveau riche [literally translated from the French meaning "new rich"] and the intellectual elites who having benefitted from the reform, became the ardent defenders of the regime. They advocate "gradual progress in a peaceful way," actually attempting to stabilize the state of passiveness and inactivity. This has the most harmful impact on the people. The problems have become much more complicated than in the eighties. We must go to the workers and peasants, make use of all legal measures to organize the masses to claim their rights and protect their security and to improve the social environment, and, during the process, change people's apathy toward the society, cultivate the ability to lead democratic lives, and develop autonomy in society.

> *The greatest mistake of the students was that they refused any compromise.*

Where has the June 4 movement left you personally?

In 1989 and the ensuing period, I was too optimistic about the situation in China. I never thought that the temptation of money and goods could have such an impact on Chinese people. I had also placed too high hopes on intellectuals and the reformist forces within the Party.

If you are in contact with any of your colleagues who remained in China, do you know what kind of impact their participation in

Tiananmen Square has had on their lives?

As far as I know, my friends in China, as well as those in exile, have not really drawn lessons from the 1989 Movement. Apathy toward politics is fairly widespread. But now we see a new force emerging among the young intellectuals who are much more highly critical and have a much more penetrating understanding of the society. In them I see hope for China.

Please tell us a little about yourself.

I joined the Communist Party in 1984. In 1951, I began my career in journalism. For advocating press freedom and muckraking, I was condemned as a Rightist [one whose political views contradict with the Party's] in 1957, and was deprived of my work as a journalist. Twenty-two years later I was rehabilitated [forced indoctrination by the Communist Party] and was able to resume my work. For the same reason, I was again expelled from the Party in 1987. In 1988 I came to the U.S., intending to return in 1989.

2

Chinese Political Reform at a Crossroads

Economist

As this article from the *Economist* points out, the ten years of economic growth that followed the Tiananmen massacre altered many people's opinions about the event. Undeniably, for most Chinese, life has improved in the 1990s. Since the crackdown, a once imposing bureaucracy has been carved away, leaving people with much more control over their lives. The economy has taken off. Jobs are chosen, not assigned. Use of new technology, such as mobile phones and computers, is widespread. Whereas in 1989 the majority reserved their greatest anger for their own government, now they direct it toward foreign critics of their country. In fact, in light of the economic failure of the former Soviet Union, some Chinese have credited their government's strong hold on power since the crackdown with the country's stability.

But not all Chinese are content to remain under an authoritarian government. A growing number of people from all walks of life want a say in who governs them and how they are governed. In addition to participative government, democracy advocates want an honest reexamination of the crackdown on Tiananmen Square, something the current government is extremely unlikely to do. To continue to succeed economically, the Chinese government must have the full support and respect of all of its citizens, many of whom want political reform as well as the economic reform they have already enjoyed. The country is at a crossroads.

S ince the bloody crackdown on June 4th 1989, China and its government have changed hugely for the better. But only when the country has dealt honestly with its past can it squarely face the future.

A decade ago, China was seething with discontent. In many cities students and workers had joined forces to protest at Communist Party corruption, and at the lack of accountability and democracy that allowed it to flourish unchecked. Now, frustration is again rising in China, but this time the anger is being turned on China's foreign critics, not its own failings.

Indeed, many thoughtful Chinese worry that mounting foreign criticism of China plays into the hands of Communist hardliners [those most likely to limit personal freedoms] opposed to any kind of political reform. Frustration is turning to despair as relations with America plummet in the wake of NATO's [accidental] bombing of China's embassy in Belgrade, China's abrupt suspension of negotiations to gain entry to the World Trade Organisation (WTO), the publication of the Cox report on China's scooping up of America's weapons secrets and, most recently, a congressional resolution condemning the Tiananmen crackdown a decade ago. "Look," says one who fell foul of the authorities back then, "Tiananmen is behind us."

Some Are Still Critical of Crackdown

Not so for some of the families who were killed when troops crushed the protest. This week the relatives of 105 of the victims took the unprecedented action of turning to the courts in support of their demand for a criminal investigation.

Among the relatives is Ding Zilin, a retired philosophy professor at Beijing University, who had kept her head firmly in her books until the day, ten years ago, when her 17-year-old son was shot dead. She has since spent her time contacting the relatives of others who died during the Tiananmen crackdown, counting the victims, and demanding an explanation, an apology and compensation from the Communist Party. This is how she describes her life now:

Since May 4th my husband and I have been blocked from leaving campus. We can walk around campus, and we can shop at the little store on the grounds, but we can't leave. How do I feel? Well, my husband and I say that this is "house arrest with Chinese characteristics". There are a dozen or more young men out-

side my house who say that if I try to leave campus they will take me away. This is like invisible violence.

The Chinese government, in other words, has not been able to put Tiananmen behind it either. The protests, officially, were deemed a "counter-revolutionary rebellion". Government leaders still insist that this was the "correct" verdict and that it will never be changed. One day presumably it will be. But for now, the events of 1989, when the Communist Party leadership visibly lost its grip and very nearly fell from power, are not up for public discussion. The year is a blank sheet in the official history. The party general secretary who fell from grace that year, Zhao Ziyang, sits under house arrest, allowed out for the occasional game of golf.

Many View Crackdown as Necessary

Time appears to be on the government's side. Many Chinese shudder at Russia's recent political and economic chaos. Where students a decade ago chanted "Give us a Gorbachev", most people today say "Thank God for Deng Xiaoping". This change was apparent in the public reaction to the NATO embassy bombing. The Tiananmen students thought they were saving a nation whose political decay seemed to put it at risk of being carved up by foreigners, as had happened in the past. On posters Deng Xiaoping was caricatured as the 19th-century empress dowager, Cixi. Last month [May 1999], by contrast, calls to maintain social stability seemed to resonate as deeply with today's students as did the government's fiercely nationalistic tone. After three days, the demonstrations outside America's embassy ended obediently.

> *Indeed, many thoughtful Chinese worry that mounting foreign criticism of China plays into the hands of Communist hardliners . . . opposed to any kind of political reform.*

As the "unofficial" verdict on Tiananmen has subtly changed over time, the government might be said to have won its propaganda campaign to depict the peaceful protests as something more. Whatever revulsion there was at the crackdown, without it, many people now say, China could not have marshalled the will to throw itself into a full-blown modernisation of the economy. Even some of those who wish democracy for China now regret the 1989 events. Their result, says one economist, was to set back democratic prospects for years.

Why Have Attitudes Changed?

To gauge just what has changed in China in the 1990s, it is worth recalling the state of the country on the eve of the protests. After ten years of "reform and opening up", China's leaders seemed to have lost the agenda. Inflation was rising, and goods of every kind were hard to find. . . . The party ruled with a casual tyranny, corrupt and nepotistic.

Frustration was perhaps highest among intellectuals, a point distilled in *Evening Chats in Beijing*, a book of conversations with Chinese intellectuals on the eve of the protests, written by a Princeton professor, Perry Link:

By 1988 . . . the questions intellectuals were raising did not have any ready answers—or any answers at all. . . . Why were we intellectuals so docile in the 1950s when Mao "criticised" us and set up his tyranny? What do we make of the "peasant consciousness" that we admired then but that oppresses us now? How can we feel certain that we have really understood the Cultural Revolution? Given the absurdity of blaming [that] on just a "gang" of only four people, what is it in all of us that allowed such violence to happen?

The questioning came at a time when economic reforms had run up against the Leninist [ideas based on the opinions of Vladimir Lenin, a Russian Communist leader] constraints of a social system that tied each person to his work-unit and that made even the most mundane activity— getting a telephone installed, buying a hot-plate, getting permission for research—a nightmarish obstacle course of petty bribes and fawning to superiors. What happened next was played out on television screens around the world (and even, for a while, in China), culminating in bloodshed as the popular mutiny, after much dithering, was put down with appalling severity.

A Growing Economy Eases Criticism

Evening chats in Beijing these days often revolve around a series of what ifs. What if the Chinese leadership had swept Tiananmen Square of students sooner? Or had established a dialogue sooner? What if the authorities had owned a few water-cannon and known about crowd control? Surely the army would then not have been ordered to fire on its own people. Once it had done so, at Deng Xiaoping's orders, the Communist Party imposed a new contract on the country: hard-fisted political control in return for a fast pace of economic modernisation.

Whatever revulsion there was at the crackdown, without it, many people now say, China could not have marshalled the will to throw itself into a full-blown modernisation of the economy.

The economic consequences are hard to exaggerate, for they represent, in many sectors, the wholesale retreat of the state. Some $200 billion of foreign investment has come to China in the past decade, and foreign-funded ventures account for over half of China's exports. The private sector now accounts for perhaps one third of the economy, up from almost nothing, and some state companies have started to act like private ones. If goods were hard to come by in 1989, today there are too many of them: consumers are spoilt for choice. Some 1.5m new fixed telephone lines are laid each month, and China will soon be the second-biggest mobile-phone market in the world. Graduates in the 1980s were told where to work. Today they dive into a competitive market. Private housing, unheard of a decade ago, is catching on. Mechanisms of state control—the household-registration system, the work-unit system, the one-child policy—have been greatly weakened. Talk in China is free, so long as it is not deemed openly to challenge the state. The new prosperity is still too unevenly spread. And wrenching change has brought the uncertainties of unemployment to many. But the greatest number of Chinese are beneficiaries, not victims.

Political Change Is Slow in Coming

But can the political system keep up with these changes, and adapt itself without violence? The Communist Party has cleaned house. More room has been made in government for younger, more meritocratic types—including June 4th protesters. The National People's Congress (NPC) takes its job of monitoring the government's performance seriously. It has also become a main centre for drafting laws, calling upon foreign legal experts for help. Under the hand of Zhu Rongji, the prime minister, central government has shrunk. A reorganisation of the central bank along regional lines is a big step towards improving economic management. A measure of competency, in other words, is spreading through the system.

The greatest number of Chinese are beneficiaries, not victims.

One of the biggest changes has come at the grassroots, where "village" democracy is now practised by the two-thirds of Chinese living in rural areas. At the top, power is no longer wielded by individuals with the stature of Mao Zedong or Deng Xiaoping, who died in 1997. Today's Politburo leaders, under the president, Jiang Zemin, need to look elsewhere for their authority. The party is fast learning the techniques of focus groups, opinion polls and complaint hotlines. Communists can learn to kiss babies, too.

Change should not be exaggerated. Power wielded at the top is still of an intensely personal kind. The inscrutable senior leadership helps give an air of stability. But there are still no mechanisms for the smooth exercise of power, or for its transfer. Lacking transparency, much of government is still choked by incompetence and corruption.

The party has bolstered its legitimacy since Tiananmen, yet that does not mean people do not want political change. Where might it come from? The democratic movement is widely written off. Its most articulate proponents—such as Fang Lizhi, Liu Binyan and Wei Jingsheng—are in exile. One exiled Tiananmen hero, Wang Dan, has come in for vituperative abuse on the Beijing University campus where he was once a hero, for daring to suggest that the embassy bombing in Belgrade might have been a genuine mistake.

Democracy Is on the Rise

Yet those who claim that real dissent has been snuffed out may underestimate the adaptability of the new democratic opposition, spearheaded by the Chinese Democracy Party.

Though two of its leaders were given stiff jail sentences last December [1998] and a score or so members have been detained in a pre-Tiananmen round-up, the party is probably much bigger than most people think—with several thousand active members around the country, drawn from all walks of life.

Besides, democracy activists have changed their tactics, if not their goals. Many seem to want to put the idea of revolution, which has driven most political change this century in China, behind them. Democrats now seek a more subtle, long-term game of participation. As one leader of the Chinese Democracy Party, Ren Wanding, argues, political change should not be pushed too far: "Just one step at a time. That way, we can nurture our democratic forces as well as give the government time to change. That's good for both sides."

Yet those who claim that real dissent has been snuffed out may underestimate the adaptability of the new democratic opposition, spearheaded by the Chinese Democratic Party.

Perhaps most intriguing is the contention by some in government that change could come swiftly, as village democracy spreads from the countryside into the cities. Once that happens, it will be hard to prevent competitive politics from taking over.

For now, though, it is hard for urbanites to grasp why swathes of the countryside have taken to elections for village leaders with such gusto. Wang Zhenyao, a senior official at the Ministry of Civil Affairs, argues that farmers have more interests that conflict with the state—and with each other. They are land-owners. They are more heavily taxed than city-dwellers. They resent those taxes when the money is badly spent or disappears into the pockets of local officials. In other words, says Mr Wang, "democracy is about interests, discussing concrete things like salaries, taxes, building roads, resolving conflicts. It's not about shouting slogans like 'Overthrow the government! Down with [the former prime minister] Li Peng!'" Farmers may understand this better than city folk, but that is changing as the state-controlled economy is dismantled. "Look at all the problems in Beijing," says Mr Wang, waving a hand to the window, "pollution, traffic chaos, construction. Democracy is about the recontrol of government. When city people say that if peasants can organise elections, we should too, I say: 'no problem.'" Wider democracy, in short, has already become the open agenda of some in government.

This suggests that a new compact between government and people may start to be redrawn sooner than many think. Indeed, in the debate over when and on what terms China should join the WTO, the western world should perhaps not exaggerate its ability to shape the course of China's political development, either for good or ill. Yet nor should it underestimate the dangers if China cannot change, or cannot change peacefully. China cannot get very far towards political reform without confronting new demands to revise the verdict on Tiananmen. But that the Communist Party will be loth to do. And it's recourse in such trying times—a prickly chauvinism—would surely be felt beyond China's borders.

3

Political Corruption Could Lead to Another Tiananmen

Bao Tong

Few people understand the political problems that sparked the Tiananmen Square Massacre better than Bao Tong, former political secretary to the Standing Committee of the Chinese Politburo and advisor to Zhao Ziyang, the Communist Party secretary ousted by the Chinese Communist Party for his leniency toward the student protesters. Bao Tong was kept in solitary confinement for seven years for his own disagreement with the party about how to handle the protests in June of 1989. In ten years, his opinions about the Tiananmen massacre have changed little. He argues in the following article that the current Chinese government must recant their political predecessors' official verdict on the protest movement of 1989, which condemned the protests as a "counterrevolutionary rebellion" rather than an honest and widespread criticism of the government. Also, he believes that current government officials must admit that the Tiananmen crackdown was wrong. If they do not do so, they are in danger of facing yet another generation of Chinese people whose dissatisfaction with government corruption—which, despite an upsurge in the economy, has changed little since the protests of 1989—might lead them to the Square yet again.

In May of 1989, as the student demonstrations continued in Tiananmen Square, and the government's internal

From "Reversing the Verdict: Chinese Dissident Reflects on Impact of Tiananmen Square Massacre, 1989," by Bao Tong, *Newsweek International*, June 7, 1999. Copyright © 1999 by Newsweek, Inc. Reprinted with permission.

splintering intensified, I had an ominous premonition that
something might happen to me. I knew that the existing
system was intolerant of the slightest nonconformity. Nevertheless, it was my firm resolution that in no circumstance
should the government crack down on the students. I decided to review the relevant paragraphs from the Constitution and the criminal-procedure laws regarding arbitrary
detention and personal freedom, which I hoped would be of
some help to me.

---

*During my endless hours in Qincheng, I
thought long and hard about the
demonstrations, and I could come to no other
conclusion than that the crackdown was wrong.*

On May 28, 1989, a week before the crackdown, I was
taken to Qincheng Prison. I immediately asked the prison
guards for copies of those laws, which they brought to me
two days later. The very next day, I used them to write my
first letter to the Communist Party Central Committee,
pointing out that it was illegal to detain me without legal
charges or a documented administrative decision. A member of the Politburo [governing body in China] sent me a
message to tell me that my letter had been passed on. I
never received a response.

The Protesters Were Justified

At the time, the only thing that I regretted was that political reform had not started earlier. I regretted that Deng
Xiaoping had decided to overturn Communist Party chief
Zhao Ziyang's proposal to resolve the crisis within democratic principles and the rule of law. But as much as I was
concerned about the negative impact that the turn of events
had for political reform, I could never have imagined that
they would actually open fire on innocent civilians. I don't
think anyone except Deng himself could have foreseen such
a thing.

During my endless hours in Qincheng, I thought long
and hard about the demonstrations, and I could come to no
other conclusion than that the crackdown was wrong. The
demonstrations that spring were not only the voice of a few

Beijing students, but expressed the concerns of all the Chinese people. They demanded democracy and an end to corruption. They wanted to ensure that the benefits of economic reform would truly go to the people and not just to government officials and their families.

The economic reforms had brought prosperity to China, but a small number of people with power and influence were reaping the greatest benefits. This was profiteering and nepotism. Only with connections could one have opportunity. The so-called market economy did not offer true competition. Without competition, there could be no transparency. This situation caused the people of China great discontent, and proved that economic reform alone is not enough. It must be accompanied by political reform as well.

Economic and Political Change Must Go Hand in Hand

After Deng's crackdown on June 4, China's policy shifted toward tighter political control but continued liberalization of the economy. The government hoped to increase public tolerance of political constraints by offering greater economic freedoms, and to use the opening of the Chinese market to undermine the international sanctions that were put in place after the crackdown. Even as this policy has gained considerable success, the question remains: how long can this last?

Economic liberalization will continue to clash with political controls. Political intolerance promotes absolute power, while economic liberalization increases opportunities. The combination creates a hotbed for corruption. In the past 10 years, the greatest benefits of economic reform have continued to go to the powerful few. The use of power in exchange for money has run rampant. Unequal opportunity and the uneven execution of the law make the vast majority of people believe that their futures are unpredictable.

As long as authoritarianism and corruption prevail, the voice of Tiananmen will continue. In the face of the growing trend of democracy around the world, even the Chinese government was finally compelled to sign the International Covenant of Civil and Political Rights (ICCPR). In today's global environment, they will find it more and more difficult to maintain their policy of political controls.

New Leaders Must Condemn the Crackdown

The Tiananmen crackdown went beyond any possible legal justification, and the principles of human rights and the spirit of democracy. If the verdict on the crackdown is not reversed, then could there be another "Tiananmen Incident"? If the government has unchecked power, it could happen again. To avoid that, the decision to crack down must be redressed.

The current leaders of China now have an opportunity to re-evaluate and surpass Deng's legacy. Most of China's current leaders were not in decision-making positions at the time of the student movement, and need not now bear the negative responsibility. But if this government isn't subject to the people's supervision and the rigors of rule of law, then the people must ask: are the government's domestic and foreign policies responsible, stable and predictable? The people have the right to demand that the leaders uphold justice and the Constitution by reassessing the 1989 movement. This is a responsibility that they cannot refuse.

If this re-evaluation comes to pass, then my time in prison will have been worthwhile.

4

The Massacre Has Emboldened Many More Chinese

Jennifer Holdaway

According to journalist Jennifer Holdaway, who writes about humans rights issues, China's political system has seen limited but significant shifts as a result of the Tiananmen Square Massacre. Though many Chinese are still either politically apathetic or fearful of reform, one of the most encouraging signs for the future has come from ordinary citizens, who instead of shunning dissidents and their families as they would have before the Tiananmen crackdown, now silently support them. Some of these citizens have broken their silence, joining with original Tiananmen protesters to actively work against an authoritarian political system they believe does not have the people's best interests at heart. Holdaway maintains that these reformists' more modest goals stand a chance of effecting lasting political change. For example, protesters no longer talk of overthrowing the Communist Party, but have sought to reform the government by working within the Chinese constitution and legal code. Also, Chinese dissidents hope to persuade government officials to reverse the verdict on the crackdown, admitting the 1989 leadership's response to protests was wrong. These challenges have emboldened the nation's huge population of workers to revitalize a workers' movement that was just beginning at the time of the Tiananmen protests. Such reform movements have gained so much legal ground, however, that the government has scrambled to write new regulations that severely limit their ability to operate.

From "China's Dissenters: What Happened Since Tiananmen," by Jennifer Holdaway, *Dissent*, Winter 1997. Copyright © 1997 by the Foundation for the Study of Independent Social Ideas, Inc. Reprinted by permission of the publisher and the author.

B eijing's repression of the 1989 protest movement and the purge that followed resulted in the death, imprisonment, or exile of thousands of Chinese. With some notable exceptions, exile organizations have foundered, losing their sense of purpose or staggering under financial scandals and internal strife. Yet inside China, many dissenters have not given up.

Since 1992, many students and intellectuals arrested in connection with the 1989 protest movement have been released, some for medical reasons and some, controversially, for "good behavior." Once out of prison, few have shown much penitence. Forced and voluntary exile have depleted their ranks, but the New York–based organization Human Rights in China currently monitors the activities of at least a hundred human rights workers in Beijing alone.

Dissidents Know Reform Takes Time

In contrast to the heady scenes in Tiananmen Square, China's dissidents today talk not of democratic revolution but of a laborious process of democratic reform in which the construction of an independent legal system, the development of civil associations, and the growth of a sense of citizenship are more important than the removal of the Communist party or particular leaders from power.

This moderation is not entirely new. Most of China's dissidents have always been reformist, and many of their current activities are an extension of trends that began before 1989. But the commitment of so many individuals to a slow and long-term struggle is a departure from the past. In spite or perhaps because of Tiananmen, more people are signing petitions, joining unofficial organizations, and challenging police and judicial abuses. Now, as the Chinese authorities embark on a new wave of repression, many are also facing detention and imprisonment.

The dissident community includes veterans of the 1978–1981 Democracy Wall movement [pro-democracy, pro-reform movement in 1978–1979 where posters were hung on a wall in Beijing] like Wei Jingsheng and Liu Nianchun, student leaders from the 1989 protest like Wang Dan, and many new recruits who have joined the movement since 1989. Diversity of age, educational background, and occupation among China's dissenters has never been greater. Here I will focus on grassroots human rights and labor activists.

Dissidents Want Reversed
Verdict on Tiananmen

One major concern of human rights activists is reversing the government's assessment of the 1989 protest movement as a "counterrevolutionary rebellion." A series of open letters and petitions has appealed for a revision of this verdict. One petition, in May 1995, was signed by forty-five prominent scientists, intellectuals, and dissidents.

In the past, relatives of dissidents rarely challenged the authorities for fear of making things worse. But last year, twenty-seven relatives of people killed on June 4 submitted a petition to the National People's Congress calling for a reassessment of the movement. One couple is now collecting the names of all those who died. Over the last few years Wei Jingsheng's sister has lobbied governments and international institutions to press for his release, and the wives of several other imprisoned dissidents have made public appeals on their behalf.

This new boldness is due partly to a massive shift in public opinion over the last fifteen years. When Wei Jingsheng was arrested in 1979, few spoke in his defense. At that time, dissenters' families were often ostracized by neighbors and co-workers. Most Chinese are still unwilling to risk their own security by speaking out, but many admire those who do. At the very least, says Hu Ping, editor of the New York–based dissident magazine *Beijing Spring*, "ordinary people no longer think people the government calls counterrevolutionaries deserve whatever they get."

Some Now Sue the State

Official sponsorship of limited legal reform is having unintended consequences. In the late 1980s . . . scholars began to lecture on the need for due process and respect for citizens' rights. Some even argued, in official and semi-official legal journals, that "counterrevolution" was a political, not a legal, concept.

Since 1989, activists have been applying these principles. . . . Until this year, there was no presumption of innocence in Chinese law, and lawyers for the accused were expected to plead only for leniency. But in 1991, lawyers for Chen Ziming and Wang Juntao, founders of an independent research organization, boldly defended their clients against the charge of being "black hands" behind the 1989 protests.

Liu Qing, who served ten years for his involvement in the Democracy Wall movement and is now chairman of Human Rights in China, reports that at least thirty people have sued the authorities for violations of their constitutional rights or the Chinese legal code. Among them is the ever-recalcitrant Wei Jingsheng. Sentenced in December 1995 to another prison term of fourteen years, he sued the Beijing police for detaining him for twenty months without trial. Liu Qing's brother, Liu Nianchun, also sued the state for a three-year "Reeducation through Labor" sentence he received in May 1996 for his role in several petitions. Liu served three years in the eighties for smuggling Liu Qing's prison memoirs out of the country.

Both Wei's and Liu's suits were recently rejected, and lawyers who have represented dissidents have met with reprisals. But the real significance of all this lies in the willingness of a growing number of Chinese to challenge the state. To a government that is used to intimidating its citizens into silence, this persistence is a disturbing trend. Even more alarming is the specter of a nascent independent workers' movement.

Workers Join the Fight

As in other "workers' states," China's official trade union, the All China Federation of Trade Unions (ACFTU), exists more to carry out government policy than to represent the working class. Since the mid-1970s, when reports of strikes in several Chinese cities filtered out, Chinese workers have increasingly resorted to independent action.

Many Democracy Wall activists were self-educated workers who drew attention to the contradiction between official ideology and real life in China's factories. Articles in their unofficial journals occasionally made admiring references to Polish Solidarity (on which the official media reported until Deng announced his support for martial law in December 1981).

Workers were punished severely for their involvement with Democracy Wall, even when their criticisms came from a Marxist perspective. Wei Jingsheng, who publicly called Deng a dictator, received a fifteen-year prison sentence. But so did Xu Wenli, a democratic socialist who regarded himself as a supporter of Deng. Shortly before his arrest, Xu had been involved in discussions with worker-activists from around the country about the possibility of starting an independent national publication.

Worker Unrest Began in Late '80s

With many of the Democracy Wall leaders in prison and others mindful of their fate, pressure for political reform came mostly from intellectual and cultural circles in the 1980s. But labor unrest increased steadily. The right to strike was deleted from the 1982 Constitution on the grounds that "contradictions" between workers and enterprises had been eliminated, but there were official reports of more than seven hundred strikes in the first ten months of 1988, one of them lasting three months.

In spite or perhaps because of Tiananmen, more people are signing petitions, joining unofficial organizations, and challenging police and judicial abuses.

In 1989, tens of thousands of workers took to the streets in sympathy with the students. At least thirty workers' organizations were formed, the largest of which, the Beijing Workers Autonomous Federation (BWAF), claimed thousands of members by the end of May. Its demands included not only wage increases and anticorruption measures but, most significantly, the right to represent workers' interests as an independent labor union.

Many ACFTU members also attended the protests, with the tacit approval of their leaders. On May 18, the organization actually donated about $25,000 to the protests while its hard-line president was out of the country. In the last days of the movement, ACFTU members also participated in meetings of the Capital Liaison Group, organized by Chen Ziming and Wang Juntao to promote dialogue among students, intellectuals, the BWAF, and other citizens' groups. Despite fierce disagreements among the participants, this group represented the government's worst nightmare—bridge-building among intellectual dissidents, workers, and other disaffected members of society.

The BWAF was short-lived, and workers were harshly punished for their role in the protests. Most of those who died on the night of June 3 were not students, but workers and ordinary citizens, and workers generally received heavier prison sentences afterward.

Unrest and Strikes Have Increased

Worker unrest has continued to rise since 1989 in response to the upheavals of government-sponsored economic reform. Wages have risen, but prices have followed them, and new workers in state-owned enterprises no longer have job security. Some estimates put unemployment at forty million in urban areas alone. Migrant workers who leave their villages to seek work in Special Economic Zones and cities are particularly vulnerable since they lack the urban residence status that would entitle them to state benefits. Estimated at over a hundred million people, many in this floating population have no access to medical care, education, or adequate housing.

Industrial safety is a widespread problem, especially in minimally regulated private operations. Safety standards have not changed since the 1950s, and there are frequent reports of fires and avoidable accidents. Government statistics, which almost certainly underestimate the problem, indicate that over twenty thousand workers were killed in industrial accidents in 1994, including more than ten thousand miners.

In 1993, the government stopped denying the reality of strikes and reported nearly ten thousand industrial actions for that year. More than twelve thousand labor disputes were reported for 1995, mostly over unpaid wages, lack of job security, and working conditions. Exiled labor leader Han Dongfang says that the official union, ACFTU, plays the good cop in these conflicts, coaxing workers back to work with promises of concessions. In fact, some of the strikers' immediate demands (usually for back pay) are often met to avoid riots, but any identifiable leaders are promptly dealt with.

Workers Attempt to Form Unions

Most of these strikes and work stoppages have been spontaneous, but there have also been several attempts to establish independent unions. In May 1992, sixteen people were arrested in connection with the clandestine Free Trade Union of China (FTUC), which called in its founding statement for the right to organize free trade unions, improved working conditions, and the release of political prisoners. In

1994, the organizers were sentenced to prison terms of between seven and twenty years, "killing the chickens for the monkeys to watch," as the Chinese say.

Subsequent organizations have sought safety in publicity. March 1994 saw the founding of the League for the Protection of the Rights of Working People, whose organizers include Liu Qing's brother, Liu Nianchun, as well as several lawyers and professors. The league welcomed not only workers, but also intellectuals, peasants, and entrepreneurs. Only "corrupt officials" were specifically excluded. A carefully worded petition submitted to the National People's Congress characterized the league as an "interest group not a political party" and called for improvements in health care and working conditions and for the restoration of the constitutional right to strike, the extension of union rights to peasants, and the disclosure of party and government officials' assets and income. Predictably, the league's attempt to register with the Ministry of Civil Affairs was rejected and several of its organizers have been arrested.

In 1993, the government stopped denying the reality of strikes and reported nearly ten thousand industrial actions for that year.

Han Dongfang, exiled leader of the BWAF and editor of the Hong Kong–based *China Labor Bulletin*, is determined to continue working for workers' rights and independent unions, even if it means going back to jail when Hong Kong reverts to Chinese rule [this happened in 1997]. Describing himself as a "real socialist," he criticizes the Communist party for permitting increasing inequality of wealth and failing to provide for workers' welfare. He is equally wary of "democrats" who say that workers must postpone their demands until economic development provides the basis for democracy. He supports the efforts of organizations such as the League for the Protection of the Rights of Working People, but insists that only protests initiated by workers can form the basis for an independent union movement.

Even before the current crackdown, China's grassroots organizers faced constant obstruction and persecution. The law permits independent associations (at least a thousand now run national operations) but severely limits the scope of their activity. To register, associations must have the approval of the "mass organization" responsible for that sector of the population (ACFTU, the All China Women's Federation, and so on). Independent groups may not duplicate the activities of official organizations, and the 1992 Trade Union Law specifically forbids the establishment of unions not affiliated with ACFTU.

Less controversial groups, including some women's rights groups, manage to circumvent these regulations by hooking up to official organizations or academic departments that are willing to provide cover. Some local branches of the All China Women's Federation also seem to pursue a somewhat independent agenda. But this is not an option for human rights and workers' organizations. Since 1989, ACFTU has shown no outward signs of disloyalty to the regime.

The government has also passed regulations against many of the dissidents' new tactics. Writings or speech harmful to "state security" is defined as "sabotage," as is the establishment of social groups or business enterprises for the same purpose. Cooperating with or accepting funds from foreign organizations is expressly forbidden.

Where none of these charges is applicable, the government continues to accuse dissidents of offenses such as hooliganism, traffic violations, and the misuse of official funds. Dissidents and their relatives are routinely arrested during international events like the UN Women's Conference or sent on "vacation" in distant provinces with a police escort. Interference with employment, marriage licenses, and resident permits is commonplace.

The Government Still Has the Upper Hand

Over the last few months the government has been flexing its muscles, arresting and sentencing many dissidents in an attempt to intimidate the rest and demonstrate its indifference to international opinion. Human Rights in China estimates that at least twenty dissidents have been sentenced this year and many more detained without trial. The student leader Wang Dan received the harshest treatment. Held in secret detention since May 1995, he was sentenced in October 1996 to an eleven-year prison term. A number of other activists fled the country, and those who remain are likely to be cautious for a while.

Although they clearly face another period of repression,

dissidents hope that the long-awaited death of Deng Xiaoping [Deng died in February of 1997] will bring a change in the political climate. But many of the obstacles they face will outlive Deng.

In rural areas, it is clan organizations, traditional religion, and secret societies that are on the rise, not human rights groups.

Although elections have been held for local-level congresses for some years now, most Chinese have little experience with democratic institutions. And despite encouraging trends such as those reported here, civil society remains weak in relation to the state. The middle class so beloved of transition theorists is still small and geographically limited. Outside urban areas, literacy levels are falling as parents take their children out of school to work and the rising cost of education puts it beyond their reach. In rural areas, it is clan organizations, traditional religion, and secret societies that are on the rise, not human rights groups.

Ironically, many who support democracy as a long-term goal espouse some variant of enlightened authoritarianism [system in which people obey a small group of people who have absolute power over them] in the short term. China's level of development, they argue, cannot support a democratic system, and only a strong central government with restrictions on popular participation can provide the stability needed for development and eventual democratization. In this construction of the options for China's future, the prosperity of Asia's newly industrializing countries is contrasted with the fragmentation and chaos of the former Soviet Union.

For those who seek social justice as well as civil rights, the odds are even more formidable. Economic reform without political accountability has caused mounting inequality and corruption as officials at all levels use their public power to accumulate private wealth. The process will be hard to reverse. Even if the transition after Deng's death is smooth and its direction liberal (neither of which is guaranteed), China's human rights and labor activists will still have plenty to do.

Important Figures in the Tiananmen Square Massacre

Bao Tong, Zhao Ziyang's secretary, who was sentenced to seven years in prison and expelled from the Chinese Communist Party for his role in the events leading up to the Tiananmen Square Massacre.

Bo Yibo, one of the Eight Elders.

Chai Ling, graduate student at Beijing University and high-ranking leader in the student protest movement.

Chen Yun, one of the Eight Elders.

Chen Zhili, Shanghai Party Committee Standing Committee member. After the massacre, he was appointed deputy secretary of the Shanghai Party Committee.

Deng Xiaoping, most powerful and respected member of the Eight Elders. He was a political leader in China at various times from the 1950s until his death in 1997.

Ding Wenjun, deputy secretary general of the Beijing Municipal Government.

Fang Lizhi, exiled professor and astrophysicist from the Chinese University of Science and Technology and the Beijing Observatory. He now teaches at the University of Arizona.

Hong Dongfang, exiled labor leader.

Hou Dejian, popular Chinese singer and participant in the hunger strikes in the square.

Hu Yaobang, deposed from his leadership role in the CCP for his ideas about economic reform, his death sparked the initial demonstrations in the square.

Jiang Zemin, Shanghai Party secretary and Politburo member. After June 4, he became party general secretary and, in 1993, was named state president.

Lao Gui, Chinese dissident and writer.

Li Peng, premier and member of the Politburo.

Li Xiannian, one of the Eight Elders.

Liu Binyan, one of China's most famous journalists who was exiled for his exposure of political corruption.

Mao Zedong, leader of China from 1949 to 1976.

Peng Zhen, one of the Eight Elders.

Qiao Shi, member of the Politburo and Party Secretariat, in charge of personnel, security, and intra-party investigation and discipline.

Wan Li, chairman of the Standing Committee of the National Peoples' Congress and member of the Politburo.

Wang Dan, leader of the Autonomous Federation of Students during the protests. Later moved to the United States.

Wang Renzhi, director of the party Propaganda Department.

Wang Zhen, one of the Eight Elders.

Wei Jingsheng, famous writer and imprisoned dissident at the time of the Tiananmen protests.

Yang Baibing, chief political commissar in the CCP.

Yang Shangkun, president of the People's Republic of China and attended the Politburo Standing Committee meetings.

Yuan Liben, secretary general of the Beijing Municipal Party Committee.

Yuan Mu, state council spokesman and close associate of Li Peng.

Zhang Gong, director of the martial law unit in Tiananmen Square before the massacre.

Zhao Ziyang, politically moderate party general secretary who was removed from his position and placed under house arrest for his failure to resolve the Tiananmen Square protests.

Zhu Rongji, mayor and deputy party secretary of Shanghai. Later became premier in Beijing and a member of the Politburo Standing Committee.

For Further Research

Books

Stephen Angle and Marina Svensson, eds., *The Chinese Human Rights Reader: Documents and Commentary, 1900–2000*. Armonk, NY: M.E. Sharpe, 2002.

Timothy Brook, *Quelling the People: Military Suppression of the Beijing Democracy Movement*. New York: Oxford University Press, 1992.

John Fairbank et al., *Children of the Dragon: The Story of the Tiananmen Massacre*. New York: Macmillan, 1990.

Human Rights in China, *Children of the Dragon: The Story of Tiananmen Square*. New York: Collier Books, 1990.

Nicholas D. Kristof and Sheryl Wudunn, *China Wakes: The Struggle for the Soul of a Rising Power*. New York: Times Books, 1994.

Liang Zhang et al., *The Tiananmen Papers: The Chinese Leadership's Decision to Use Force Against Their Own People—In Their Own Words*. New York: Public Affairs, 2001.

James Miles, *Legacy of Tiananmen: China in Disarray*. Ann Arbor: University of Michigan Press, 1996.

Photographers and reporters of the *Ming Pao News, June Four: A Chronicle of the Chinese Democratic Uprising*. Fayetteville: University of Arkansas Press, 1989.

Tony Saich, ed., *The Chinese People's Movement: Perspectives on Spring 1989*. Armonk, NY: M.E. Sharpe, 1990.

Harrison E. Salisbury, *Tiananmen Diary: 13 Days in June*. Boston: Little, Brown, 1989.

Orville Schell, *Mandate of Heaven: The Legacy of Tiananmen Square and the Next Generation of China's Leaders*. New York: Simon and Schuster, 1995.

Shen Tong with Marianne Yen, *Almost a Revolution*. Boston: Houghton Mifflin, 1990.

Sui-Sheng Chao and Suisheng Zhao, eds., *China and Democracy: The Prospect for a Democratic China*. New York: Routledge, 2000.

Yi Mu and Mark V. Thompson, *Crisis at Tiananmen: Reform and Reality in Modern China*. San Francisco: China Books and Periodicals, 1989.

Periodicals

Melissa August et al., "Ten Years After Tiananmen," *Time*, May 31, 1999.

Sophie Beach, "Tiananmen Plus Ten," *Nation*, June 14, 1999.

Todd Carrel, "Beijing," *National Geographic*, June 12, 1999.

Pico Iyer, "The Unknown Rebel," *Time*, April 13, 1998.

Robert A. Manning, "China Closet: Facing the Legacy of Tiananmen," *New Republic*, July 20, 1998.

Andrew J. Nathan, "The Tiananmen Papers," *Foreign Affairs*, January/February 2001.

George Wehrfritz, "Rethinking Tiananmen: The Nation's Newest Leaders Re-Examine the Past," *Newsweek*, March 10, 1997.

Index

83–84
families of, 96–97, 109
government response to, 15–16
hunger strike by, 42–45
portrayal by CPC and PLA, 55–56,
  63–64, 66–68
prior to uprising, 13–15
workers as, 73
see also peasants; reform movement;
  students; workers (laobaixing)
public funds, 25–26
public opinion (Chinese)
  of Deng, 97
  of government, 29–31, 37, 81, 110
  Jochnowitz on, 33–35
  of massacre, 96–98

Qiang, Kenneth, 79
Qiao Shi, 46, 49

reform movement, 93–94, 100–102,
  107, 109–10
see also democracy; economy
religion, 22, 115
Ren Wanding, 88, 101
Restrepo, Juan, 82, 83
Rosett, Claudia, 82
Roth, Richard, 81, 82
rumors
  of journalists' deaths, 81–82
  People's Liberation Army on, 59–60
Russia, 97

San Francisco Examiner (newspaper), 82
Self-Government Union of College
  Students, 62
Sheng Xue, 85–88
Simpson, John, 77, 79, 82–83
Small Group to Research Reform of
  the Central Political System, 13
socialism, 14, 35
see also Communist Party of China
soldiers. *See* People's Liberation Army
South China Morning Post (newspaper),
  75
Standing Committee of the Chinese
  Politburo, 103
State Education Commission, 14
State Statistical Bureau, 26
strikes, 112
see also protesters; unions
students, 73–74
  demands of, 14–15, 45
  goals of, 91
  Liu on self-defeating movement of,
    90–94
  Qiao on, 49
  response to People's Liberation
    Army, 53

and workers, 36
see also protesters
surveys, 14
survivors, 85–88
see also protesters

Television Española, 82, 83
Tiananmen Square, 10
  on anniversaries of massacre, 88
  hunger strike in, 14–15, 42–45
  media reports from, 71, 77–84
  People's Liberation Army on death
    toll in, 60
  size of, 76–77
  warning announcements in, 60–61,
    77–78
see also massacre; People's Liberation
  Army (PLA)
Trade Union Law (1992), 114

unions, 110–15
  Deng on, 39–41
  Zhang on, 62
see also individual names of unions
United States, 21–22, 53, 96

Walters, Barbara, 84
Wang Dan, 88, 100, 102, 114
Wang Juntao, 109, 111
Wang Zhen, 25, 49
Wang Zhenyao, 101
Washington Post (newspaper), 82
Wasserman, Tony, 78
weapons, 67, 76
Wei Jingsheng, 100, 108, 109
Western culture, 21–22
Williams, Derek, 78, 80–82
workers (*laobaixing*), 70, 71
  harmed by economic reform, 12
  strikes by, 112
  and students, 36
  as threat to government, 73
  treatment by students of, 90–94
see also unions
World Trade Organization (WTO),
  96
Wuer Kaixi, 82

Xu Wenli, 110

Yang Baibang, 75
Yang Shangkun, 25, 48
Yao Yilin, 46
Yuan Liben, 56, 64–65
Yuan Mu
  casualties estimated by, 56–57
  on media coverage, 55, 58–59
  on protesters, 64–69
Yu Shuo, 83–84

Zhang Gong, 56
  on civilian casualties, 63–64
  on People's Liberation Army, 60–63
  on rumors about massacre, 59–60
Zhang Jin, 85, 87–88
Zhao Ziyang, 11, 14, 15
  Bao on, 103–106

ideology of, 12–13
imprisonment of, 97
Liu on, 21
on martial law, 46–48
resignation of, 16–17, 92
Zhu Rongji, 100

	DATE DUE		